Banishing Bullying Behavior

q/10

Banishing Bullying Behavior

Transforming the Culture of Pain, Rage, and Revenge

SuEllen Fried and Blanche Sosland

ROWMAN & LITTLEFIELD EDUCATION

A division of

ROWMAN & LITTLEFIELD PUBLISHERS, INC.
Lanham • New York • Toronto • Plymouth, UK

PUBLISHED BY ROWMAN & LITTLEFIELD EDUCATION

A division of Rowman & Littlefield Publishers, Inc.
A wholly owned subsidiary of The Rowman & Littlefield Publishing Group, Inc.
4501 Forbes Boulevard, Suite 200, Lanham, Maryland 20706
http://www.rowmaneducation.com

Estover Road
Plymouth PL6 7PY
United Kingdom

British Library Cataloguing in Publication Information Available

Library of Congress Cataloging-in-Publication Data

Fried, SuEllen.
  Banishing bullying behavior : transforming the culture of pain, rage and revenge / by
SuEllen Fried and Blanche Sosland.
    p. cm.
  Includes bibliographical references and index.
  ISBN 978-1-60709-220-9 (cloth : alk. paper) — ISBN 978-1-60709-221-6 (pbk. : alk.
paper) — ISBN 978-1-60709-222-3 (electronic)
    1. Bullying in schools—Prevention.   2. School violence—Prevention.   3. School
      children—Conduct of life.
  I. Sosland, Blanche E. (Blanche Eisemann), 1936-
  II. Title.
  LB3013.3.F748 2009
  371.5'8—dc22   2009031958

Printed in the United States of America

∞ TM The paper used in this publication meets the minimum requirements of American
National Standard for Information Sciences—Permanence of Paper for Printed Library
Materials, ANSI/NISO Z39.48-1992.

Contents

Acknowledgments

Blanche Sosland, my co-author has been a blessing to work with on this collaboration. Her instincts were always right on target. Her expertise as a former Director of Teacher Education at Park University added an invaluable dimension and her passion for children with special needs resulted in an important chapter. Blanche's longstanding belief in the effectiveness of my work has been a source of immeasurable support. The Sosland family is beloved in our community and members of her family, especially David and Abby, were indispensable to our final product.

My husband, Harvey, rose to every occasion of my infinite needs. His "being there for me" was limitless. He continues to be the irreplaceable anchor in my life. Blanche and I drew heavily on the work that Paula Fried, our daughter, had contributed to two previous books on this topic that she co-authored with me. *Bullies, Targets & Witnesses,* published in 2003 by M.Evans and Co, in particular, was a source of significant content.

Our son, Jeff, CEO of Beebe Medical Center, in Delaware sponsored several training opportunities for me and our other son, Marc, who is an attorney, shared some crucial legal advice. Our seven "miracles" (our grandchildren) provided personal information scattered throughout our book. I am so proud of Elise Stuewe, Samantha Fried, Joe Fried, Jim Fried, Sam Stuewe and deeply grateful for the special material from Allison Stuewe and Anne Fried. Camille Fried, my daughter-in-law and an extraordinary fifth grade teacher at Tillman Elementary School in Kirkwood, MO., is a resource I turn to, time and time again. Her principal, B.R. Rhoads, critiqued material and his recommendations added considerably to the value of our work.

Betty Barker Bashaw, a cherished friend and respected psychiatrist, shared significant information and essential research. She never failed to find ways to be helpful to me. My BullySafeUSA Certified Trainers—Dixie Dakos, Mary Fischer, Jan Klein, Lynne Lang, Vicki Price, Kathleen Saucier, and Deborah Trust were crucial consultants for the Chapter on Burning Questions from Educators. Debbie Johnston is an awesome advocate for bullying prevention. She is a role model for all of us.

Mary Fischer, Kathy Saucier and Lynne Lang provided significant work toward my evaluation results. Andrew Terranova, Ph.D., tracked my program for many years, through untimely hurricanes in New Orleans and Ft. Myers, Florida. I can never adequately express my appreciation for his professional participation and persistence. Judy Pfannenstiel provided valuable expertise and time to complete the data analysis for my evaluation.

It has been a pleasure to work with Rowman & Littlefield Education. Tom Koerner's response to our idea for this book was immediate and sustaining. His sound advice served us well as our book evolved. Maera Stratton was always available when needed and expanded our thinking about our roles as co-authors. Lynda Phung brought all the pieces together and skillfully guided us through the production stage. Rita Blitt and Norman Polsky have given national and international visibility to the concept of kindness and I have benefited greatly from their creativity and generosity. Robert Goodman continued to be my technology guru as I faced computer challenges.

A cherished group of women friends for thirty years, known as the "Watering Hole," bring me such joy and now research proves that they are adding years to my life, as well.

Sandra Fabian, with Children's Hospital of the King's Daughters invited me to work in Norfolk, Virginia, where I learned as much as I taught. Teresa Greenberg shared a most pertinent story and Molly Laflin continues to send me resource information I would never have discovered. Mariner Kemper, CEO of UMB Bank is trying to ensure that my program will reach as many children as possible. His belief in my ability is a continuing source of cherished encouragement.

Members of Reaching Out From Within, an inmate self-help program in twelve Kansas Correctional Facilities not only provided me with authentic anecdotal material, they continue to be a weekly source of inspiration to me.

Brad Slaughter and Mark Schotte, of Bark Productions, Kansas City, MO produced my training DVD. They assembled a first rate crew and made an invaluable contribution. I am profoundly grateful for the role they played in making this training film possible.

Dr. Linda Tinsley, principal of Blue-Jacket Flint Elementary School in Shawnee, Kansas, is an awesome principal. Dr. Tinsley graciously allowed me to use her school as our production site. One of her marvelous fifth grade teachers, Killeen Koontz, put her wonderful students in my hands for the filming.

Malcolm Gladwell's book, *The Tipping Point,* had a profound effect on my search for practical, innovative strategies to bring about social change. No matter how daunting the future appears, he is a persuasive advocate for possibility. What a gift to a world holding its breath!

Had it not been for Irving Sloan, I might never have been a published author. Irv was a legendary teacher at Scarsdale Middle School, Scarsdale, NY; an author; a social justice champion; and a dear friend who died in 2008. I am just one of countless people who claim him as a potent influence. I miss him terribly.

SuEllen Fried

There was no text in over twenty years of college and university teaching that my students appreciated as much as *Bullies and Victims* by SuEllen and Paula Fried. Keenly aware of the lack of proper preparation for teachers to deal with the ever-growing challenge of bullying in the classroom I contacted SuEllen Fried to ask her if my students could observe her conducting a Student Empowerment Session. This was an enormously successful experience for my students and both SuEllen and I agreed that there was a tremendous need for a text in higher education to prepare classroom teachers to adequately meet the needs of their students to banish bullying.

When we presented our proposal for such a text to our editor Tom Koerner, he, in his infinite wisdom, saw the need for a much broader readership. I am most grateful for Tom's encouragement and guidance throughout. Literally hundreds of people who heard that I was working on this book, professionals, parents, strangers echoed Tom's belief in the need for this book and everyone had his or her own bullying story to share.

My sincere thanks to Maera Winters, editorial assistant, for her ready answers to our many questions.

I am most grateful for opportunity both on a professional level and a personal level to have co-authored SuEllen's third book on peer abuse, a subject we both feel passionately about. I think our passion grew almost daily as we worked on our manuscript.

I was truly blessed to grow up in a home filled with unconditional love. Both of my parents encouraged excellence in whatever we pursued and took enormous pride in our accomplishments. My sister Ruth Fost and I share the strong belief that we are who we are because of what we learned from our Mother, Kate Simon Eisemann, both in the areas of parenting and professionalism. She was at least 60 years ahead of her time as a woman who combined career and parenting, who modeled caring, empathy and kindness in everything she did. She received a lot of teasing for her insistence on healthy eating, good nutrition, daily exercise, and care of the environment.

My gratitude goes to Dr. Warren Wheelock who was a wonderful mentor from the beginning of graduate school through my doctoral program and beyond. After all these years he still had the answer to any question I had during the writing of this book.

I am most grateful to Dr. LaDonna Ebright, assistant professor of early childhood education at Park University, for her insightful reading of our early chapters.

Many thanks to Pat Antonopolos, Joe Tumbler, Marla Kash, Matthew Rudzik, and Deborah Howard who each in their own way made a meaningful contribution and enabled me to co-author this book.

I would like to thank my cousin, Dr. Gus Eisemann, who has been more like a brother and wonderful friend for his encouragement, support, and always "being there" for every member of my family. It was also nice to share the experience of working on manuscripts at the same time.

It would take much more space than I have to adequately thank my husband, Neil, children, children by marriage, and grandchildren for their unconditional love, encouragement, and support. They have earned my highest respect for "giving back" to their respective communities in the areas of education, health issues, the arts, the environment, and religious institutions.

My appreciation to Jeffrey for guiding us through the preliminary steps of publishing based on his experience as the author of *Cooperating Rivals—The Riparian Politics of the Jordan River Basin* and to David for his much needed technical assistance all along the way on this project as well as with many of my endeavors. Special thanks to Abby, who in spite of her very busy schedule volunteered to read this manuscript. By sharing her talent and experience as a writer she made significant contributions to the final draft of this book. My gratitude to Debbie, whose support of my professional pursuits started when she was in kindergarten and told her class that her mother was an artist (I was taking an oil painting class on my "night out") and has continued through these many years.

Thank you, Josh, for sharing your memory of being bullied walking home from kindergarten almost 45 years ago. You personify the fact that children often do not tell their parents about being bullied and yet the memories remain vivid for such a long time.

Neil is the quintessential husband and best friend. He also provided excellent technical assistance whenever needed. I feel truly blessed by the full life, never a dull moment, we have been able to share.

Blanche Sosland

Foreword

While there are fewer than 100 child fatalities each year at school, literally millions of kids suffer from physical and emotional violence in the form of bullying, harassment, stalking, intimidation, humiliation, and fear. Beyond the rare events of gun shots at school are the common events of psychological stabbings—the millions of kids who suffer emotional daggers to their hearts at school. Sticks and stones and bullets may break their bones, but words can break their hearts.

Banishing Bullying Behavior comes at a time when our national consciousness about the nature and consequences of bullying in schools has risen. But it has been a painful raising process. It was not until the outbreak of school shootings in our country during the 1990s that bullying took its rightful place as a serious issue with far-reaching consequences. Research from the FBI and academic social scientists demonstrated the central role of being bullied in the psychology of youth who reached a breaking point and responded with murderous rage. This recognition led to a new generation of research and programmatic action. We learned that far from being the benign inconvenience some portrayed or the character-building "toughening" that others claimed to see, bullying is traumatic and destructive. We learned that adults charged with the responsibility of building positive social environments in schools are responsible for bullying and preventing it. We learned that mobilizing students to set high standards of caring for their fellows is the best way to prevent bullying. We learned that we need not a "war on bullying," but policies and practices that "make peace with kids."

SuEllen Fried and her colleague Blanche Sosland have brought heart and head to bear in this book. They offer a thoughtful analysis, communicate compassion for targets and perpetrators alike, and explore programmatic efforts to make schools more positive places for children and youth. They reach out to educators, parents, support staff, concerned citizens, and kids themselves in this effort, with guidance. Their book focuses on how the social system of the school plays a decisive role in the process of bullying, sexual harassment, and emotional violence in the lives of children and youth. It includes analyses of special themes for parents, teenagers, and professionals. For example, for parents, an important theme is the need to accept the reality that there is bullying, harassment, and emotional violence in today's schools and use this awareness to form an alliance with other concerned parents and approach the school system together, starting with the principal. For kids, the message is that they should not have to take on too much themselves; dealing with bullying, sexual harassment, and emotional violence at school is first and foremost an adult responsibility but one in which kids can play a role. Indeed, research shows that the actions of witnesses are critical in whether or not bullying flourishes or withers in a school.

For the professional, the message is to avoid the temptation to see bullying as a personal problem and instead to always look for the workings of the school as a social system. This implies strategies for responding that include character education, better feedback from students, and more explicit demonstration of adult caring in the school. The goal is policies and programs that seek to change the culture of the school. As I see it, expecting to replace bullying with nurturance and peace without changing school climate is unrealistic. It is like claiming to be on a diet and going to MacDonald's and eating three Big Macs and two apple pies and seeking to balance this out by drinking a Diet Coke. No, programming to deal with bullying is predicated on efforts to create a more peaceful and supportive school. SuEllen Fried and Blanche Sosland have served up a well balanced "meal" here for those who care for kids and seek to bring peace and justice to the world they inhabit day after day, month after month, year after year during the first two decades of life.

James Garbarino, PhD
Director, Center for the
Human Rights of Children
Loyola University Chicago

Preface

It is no sin to attempt and fail, the only sin is to fail to make the attempt.

—SuEllen Fried

Bullying is not static. Over the years, our awareness and our beliefs have gone through many stages. There was a time when we believed that only boys were bullies. There was a time when we believed that bullying was confined to a fist fight or a beating. There was a time when we believed that bullying was a rite of passage for all children. Today we have given up every one of those beliefs and more are going by the board with each passing day. The impact of technology and cyber bullying has added a whole new dimension to peer abuse.

Writing this book in 2008 and 2009 has been a time of tumultuous, devastating change on so many fronts. The Chinese figure for crisis is a combination of danger and opportunity. We believe that the crises we face today offer enormous opportunities to rethink some of our cherished ideas and to replace them with concepts that will sustain us in this post-catastrophic era.

Our collaboration began out of our mutual concern for two major issues. One is our anguish about the countless number of children who are being tormented and abused by their peers. We have heard too many heartbreaking stories about students at the mercy of shameless classmates. How can we stand by and allow our young, hopeful children to have their spirits mangled so thoughtlessly? And how can we allow such hurtful children to have so much power? Power that will be detrimental to *their* well-being, as well.

The other is our unwillingness, to date, to support and provide the quantity and quality educators that our children deserve. We marvel at Singapore, where they are investing in teacher's abilities to teach a curriculum focused on critical thinking and inquiry—skills needed in a high tech-economy. Teachers are recruited from the top third of each graduating high school class into a fully paid four-year teacher education program. When they enter the profession, teachers' salaries are higher than those of beginning doctors. This information comes from a fascinating article about teacher investment in countries abroad by Linda Darling Hammond, the Charles E. Ducommun professor of education at Stanford University, cited in our references.

We have partnered to bring fresh perspectives to a topic that now enjoys a tremendous amount of interest and concern. If you Google the term *bullying,* you will discover an endless list of links. Though the beginning of our book relies heavily on basic information drawn from *Bullies, Targets & Witnesses—Helping Children Break the Pain Chain,* we have used that foundation to take us into the future with new ideas, resources, and concrete strategies.

Some information is referenced in several chapters. For example, cyber bullying information is discussed in numerous chapters.

More and more children with special needs are entering our school system and deserve serious attention as it relates to bullying. More families under financial stress need support and compassion from our society. A distorted value system has taken us into a spiral of economic hardship. The time is ripe to create a culture of caring—for children, for families, for humanity.

We are convinced that childhood bullying infects a much broader playing field than the playground. All bullying behaviors must be banished, beginning in early childhood. Left to fester, there will be toxic consequences.

It will take Change Agents—a tipping point of children, educators, parents, prisoners, policy makers, and citizens to create a culture of caring. There will never be a better time to begin the change we envision.

Chapter 1

The Dynamics of Pain, Rage, and Revenge

I don't blame those kids for wanting to get back at those guys. It was horrible the way they were treated—day after day, after day.

—Maury, a student

DYNAMICS OF BULLYING

After many years of listening to students talk about abuse from their peers, and reading so many reports of students who had taken weapons to their schools and deliberately killed their classmates, SuEllen Fried kept wondering what could be learned from this tragic pattern. Oftentimes, blameless students who had never bullied the enraged shooters and might have even tried to befriend them, became victims. Beloved teachers who sacrificed their lives trying to protect students took bullets, as well. There seemed to be no way to make sense of the horrifying trail of school shootings.

These shocking student killings have taken place in Japan, Germany, and other countries, as well. Beyond explanations about children having easy access to guns, the influence of violent media and the fears of copycat behavior, Fried searched for a root that would cover the random and the specific. She ultimately developed a theory that she believes is the dynamic of bullying—the cycle of pain, rage, and revenge. (See figure 3.1)

The cycle begins when pain is inflicted and anger begins to simmer. Anger is a state of extreme displeasure, which is a normal emotion and suggests no level of intensity. There are many ways to control anger, or at least defuse it. There are anger management courses, therapy groups, many books and

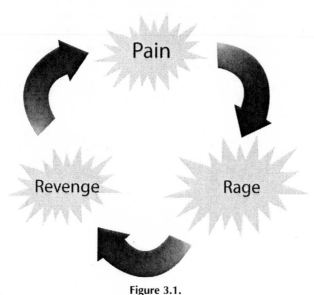

Figure 3.1.

self help resources for people to deal with their anger but anger can turn to rage when the intensity reaches a level that is unbridled and less likely to be checked.

Consider the connection between the amount of pain and the intensity of the anger. Imagine a young person who is confronted daily with ridicule and humiliation, with torment and physical abuse, with isolation and ostracism from his/her peers. Combine this with duration of time, an increasing level of contempt, an insurmountable balance of power, a lack of protection from adults in authority and we can understand how the anger accumulates and can turn to rage. Especially when they are exposed to dysfunctional parental role models and a profusion of media images that portray seething anger.

When enough rage collects, young people are consumed with thoughts of revenge. Enraged student becomes preoccupied with thoughts of retaliation and the only kind of reasoning that survives, is planning for the retribution. Even well thought-out plans cannot always anticipate the chaos that follows. At such moments, the craving for vengeance supersedes the pre-conceived plan. Victims become not only those who were responsible for the actual acts of cruelty, or those who looked on with derision or silence but for those who are at hand. The rage can even take on an entire system.

The violence that erupts causes enormous pain, and the cycle begins again. The pattern often continues into adulthood and escalates into the global conflicts that we are much too familiar with today. Many wars between tribes, countries, regions, and religions can be traced back to pain.

There are countless examples in history where a violation of cultural rules, an invasion of land or a murder set off a reactive aggression. The revenge then takes on a force of its own and the cycle gets stuck in the revenge stage. With the passage of time, sometimes the source of the original pain becomes lost, even to the combatants.

It is important to remind ourselves, again, that the students who brought guns to school and killed their classmates and teachers were not the bullies who intimidated their peers. They were the young people, the targets, who absorbed the pain and reached a breaking point where only revenge could satisfy their rage. This statement is not meant to justify their behavior; it is only to underscore the consequence of ignoring their pain.

One day, after drawing this cycle of pain, rage and revenge on a blackboard and explaining it to a middle school audience, a student came up and suggested that another cycle might be appropriate for many children. He reported that he definitely understood the "pain" part, but that it didn't evolve into rage and revenge for him. Aggression was not comfortable for him. He described how the pain he experienced caused him to be depressed and he had considered committing suicide on many occasions. The only factor that prevented him from taking his own life, he confided, was thinking about the pain it would cause for his parents. He suggested the following cycle. (See figure 3.2).

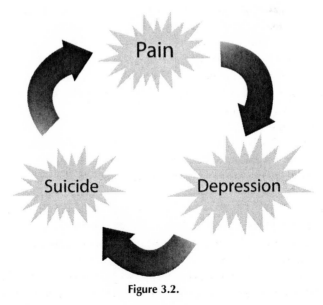

Figure 3.2.

When the pain is turned inward, it can lead to depression. Depression is an indication of anger that has been repressed. The most positive strategy for all of us is to prevent pain whenever possible. Even when the pain occurs, there are opportunities for healing and dealing with the anger—whether it is overt or suppressed. The longer it rankles, however, the more it tends to calcify and become resistant to a solution.

More recently, after drawing both cycles on a blackboard at a Midwestern middle school, a student politely introduced himself at the end of the session and shared that he moves back and forth between these two cycles of pain. Some days he comes to school enraged and plots ways to get back at the students who make his life miserable because he is overweight. Other days, he just feels like giving up and contemplates the easiest way to do away with himself. This confession led to the in figure 3.3 illustration.

Some students, such as Eric Harris and Dylan Klebold, who killed 12 students and a teacher at Columbine High School in Littleton, Colorado, and Seung-Hui Cho, the student at Virginia Tech, in Blacksburg, Virginia who killed 32 people, do both—kill their classmates, teachers, and then turn their guns on themselves. In both of these cases, efforts to find an explanation led to a history of peer rejection. In the case of Seung-Hui Cho, there were students and teachers at Virginia Tech who sensed his loneliness and attempted to reach out to him. It appears, however, that the early rejection he experienced left him with scars too deep to be put to rest. He transferred his long-held rage to the University, a system that was not the source of his pain.

These tragedies are all the more reason for us to impress upon young children the need to stop the pain of others whenever possible. It is equally imperative for adults to intervene quickly and consistently when they observe or learn about childhood bullying. Just because students are not acting out in some visible way or screaming at their abusers, does not mean they are not suffering. We cannot assume that the absence of expressed distress implies the absence of a problem.

This is an appropriate place to share a lesson learned at a prison in Kansas. It is not about violence, it is about cognitive behavior. Fried is involved in a prison program called Reaching Out From Within, a self-help program for inmates in seven correctional facilities in Kansas. Twelve groups of men and women meet weekly in various levels of minimum, medium and maximum-security units. At each meeting, one inmate is assigned to facilitate a discussion on a topic of interest such as child abuse, spouse abuse, substance abuse, sexual abuse, anger management, forgiveness and various other topics that deal with the roots of violence.

One evening Fried attended a meeting at the maximum-security unit of one of the penitentiaries. The topic of the evening was Cognitive Behavior.

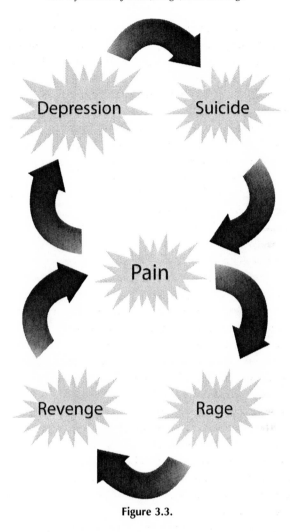

Figure 3.3.

Ronnie, the inmate chairman of the group was facilitating the meeting. Ronnie began by writing a few words on the blackboard in a prison classroom. He scratched out the words—attitudes, feelings, behavior. Then he turned to the group and said that he could draw a lot of graphs and charts but he preferred to make the lesson as relevant as possible, so he asked if there was anyone in the group that had had a conflict of any kind in the past week.

Rick raised his hand. "Two days ago I got written up for a discipline charge by a guard and I am still furious," he said. Ronnie approached him and asked him why he had been written up. Rick replied that another inmate who was a Muslim had an extra prayer rug and gave it to him, even though he, Rick, was not a Muslim. He was happy to have a rug under his feet when he rolled out of his bunk on the cold, concrete floor in the morning. The guard in question stopped by the cell and asked Rick where he got the rug. He made up some story, which the guard later checked out and gave him a write-up for lying.

Ronnie looked at Rick and asked him if he knew that lying to a guard was cause for a write-up. Rick started ranting about the guard and how she always looked for any excuse to write up an inmate and went on and on about the guard.

Ronnie calmly repeated the questions: "Rick, do you know that if you lie to a guard you will get written up?" Rick kept ranting and Ronnie kept repeating the question until Rick finally admitted that he knew the rule. Ronnie then asked Rick, "Why did you lie to the guard?" Rick was clearly upset that he was getting no sympathy for his punishment and in complete exasperation he yelled: "Because the system sucks and the guards suck and I am not going to tell them anything!"

At that point, Ronnie turned to the group, thanked Rick for illustrating the point of the session and stated "Belief trumps reason."

"Belief trumps reason" happens more frequently than we realize. If we *believe* that bullying is a childhood pattern of behavior that all children participate in and that if we, adults, just leave things alone, kids will work it out, we are trumping reason. If we *believe* that because we are not observing bullying, it must not be occurring, we are trumping reason. If we *believe* something hurtful was truly happening, one of the students would tell us, we are trumping reason.

A sense of relief that abuse isn't happening, can turn into a belief. That is why it is so important for adults to be vigilant.

The pain factor in all of deliberations on this theory was most succinctly and purely expressed by a young girl who waited patiently in line at the conclusion of a school assembly to tell me something she had learned in Sunday School. "Hurt people, hurt people" she said softly and rushed away to her next class. Her tone of voice revealed that "hurt" was first an adjective and then, a verb.

Hurt people, hurt people—so simple, yet so profound. How can we discover these crevices of pain that lurk inside of our children's souls?

A study by the U.S. Secret Service in the fall of 2000 found that in two-thirds of the thirty-seven school shootings since 1974, the attackers felt "persecuted, bullied, threatened, attacked or injured." *Time* magazine, in a May 28, 2001, article, "Voices From The Cell," documented the imprisonment of twelve male teens who killed teachers, students, parents, and/or wounded over 50 others. According to the article by Timothy Roche, "Almost all the shooters were expressing rage, either against a particular person for a particular affront or, more often against a whole cohort of bullying classmates." One of the teen prisoners told a psychiatrist that he felt that going to prison would be better than continuing to endure the bullying at school.

A high school student in the Northeast left school one afternoon, slid into the seat of his pickup truck, put a gun to his head, and fired a deadly bullet. Before killing himself, he left a note addressed to the three boys who had bullied him relentlessly. He wrote: "I feel sorry for you because you are going to remember what I did for the rest of your lives."

Then there is the case of Andy Williams, the fifteen-year-old student at Santana High School in California, who killed two students and wounded thirteen other people. His classmates had taunted him because of his small size, pale complexion, and high voice. Students would regularly beat him up and call him a "pussy." Following his arrest, Andy told investigators he planned to run away and kill himself after the shooting. Instead, he will spend fifty years in prison—three years in a juvenile prison and forty-seven years in a maximum-security facility. Was there anyone in his school who knew about the bullying? Were there any witnesses who could have intervened in his behalf or alerted adults? Was there anyone who could have changed the outcome for all concerned?

Chapter 2

Dimensions and Overview of Bullying

In the past few years there have been many school shootings. I think this is due to them kids getting picked on and not let into groups."

—Jeremy, a student

DIMENSIONS AND OVERVIEW OF BULLYING

Are there some valuable life lessons that children can learn from bullying experiences or is bullying always negative? Is bullying more severe today than it was fifty years ago? Is there a correlation between bullying and other serious social problems? Is bullying a childhood rite of passage or is it a form of child abuse? We will explore these questions in this chapter.

It took SuEllen Fried and her daughter, Paula Fried, nearly two years to find a publisher for their first book, *Bullies & Victims—Helping Your Child Through the Schoolyard Battlefield,* in 1996. Bullying was dismissed as a subject without substance or appeal—a childhood rite of passage that is a perennial part of growing up.

However, when radio interviews followed publication, adults flooded the call-in shows. One caller cited vivid childhood memories of kids ganging up on someone with fists, bats, and bicycle chains and claimed that bullying is an important learning experience about how to defend oneself. Most of the callers, however, recounted painful taunts that linger and sting though many years have passed. Some callers spoke of suicidal thoughts, dysfunctional marriages, the inability to make a commitment to a partner, failed businesses—all directly related to the circumstances of childhood bullying.

The truth is, bullying was horrendous then and it's become lethal now. As we have journeyed into the twenty-first century, seared with tragic images of students fleeing schools, sobbing in each other's arms, imprinted with the haunting faces of anguished parents, can we doubt that bullying is excruciatingly different from the world of fifty years ago?

Half a century ago it was unthinkable that a child would come to school with a gun and deliberately take the lives of classmates and teachers. School shootings have become a fact of life, and yet, countless school administrators have not begun to put comprehensive antibullying plans in place.

The National Youth Violence Prevention Resource Center reports that over 5.7 million students are estimated to be involved in bullying as either a bully, a target of bullying, or both. Thirteen percent reported that they bullied others, 11 percent were the target of bullying, and 6 percent were both bullies and targets.

A telephone survey, "Talking with Kids about Tough Issues"—reported that 74 percent of eight to eleven years olds said teasing and bullying occur at their school, more than the incidence of smoking, drinking, drugs, or sex. The rate increased to 86 percent among children aged twelve to fifteen years old.

The National Education Association estimates that every seven minutes of every school day, a child is the victim of bullying, and 85% of the time there is no intervention by other students or adults. Over 280,000 students are physically attacked each month at high schools. One third of all students say they've heard another student threaten to kill someone. One in five reports they know someone who brought a gun to school. Even so, teachers and school administrators tend to underestimate the problem, which peaks in middle school.

Is bullying an inevitable part of growing up? Does it toughen kids up, teach them how to handle unexpected conflicts, and make the transition from childhood to adulthood easier to negotiate? Or is it a traumatic power struggle between youthful, unequal parties—a form of unlabeled child abuse?

Alyssa George, Miss Kansas 2007, a beautiful and bright young woman from a small Kansas community, was a target of bullying during all of her public school years. She was an athlete, a scholar, a talented musician, and extremely attractive. She was painfully ostracized and isolated by her classmates and, no matter how hard she tried, was never able to convert their rejection. Her mother repeatedly assured her that the problem was not with Alyssa but with the children who could not handle her many accomplishments. It was not until college, when she joined a sorority, that she experienced the novel joy of friendship—a bond that so many take for granted.

In the competition for Miss Kansas, all candidates were required to choose a platform that they would espouse should they be selected. Alyssa chose bullying prevention as her theme and spent a frenetically scheduled year, traveling all across the state making appearances at hundreds of school assemblies and having a powerful impact on thousands and thousands of students. She turned her bullying experience into an amazing calling. She not only touched students' hearts, she affected their behavior with her savvy, engaging style and presentation.

Did bullying "toughen her up?" Did it teach her how to hold on to her self-concept when others were determined to tear it down? Will it prove to be a valuable part of her life? It has often been said that what doesn't destroy us makes us stronger, but we believe that a lesson learned at such emotional expense cannot justify the tolerance of bullying.

SuEllen Fried and Blanche Sosland, Ph.D., have been engaged in antibullying work for more than fifteen years. Fried has facilitated student empowerment sessions with over 85,000 students; conducted in-service training for thousands of educators, counselors, and administrators; and presented seminars to parents and child advocates all across the country. Dr. Sosland was a member of the Department of Education at Park University from 1979 to 2000, and served as chairman for a number of years, training thousands of future educators.

Based on their bullying prevention work over these many years, Fried and Sosland maintain that bullying is a form of child abuse—peer abuse. If a child is hurting, it doesn't matter if the perpetrator is a parent or a peer. If a child is suffering, it doesn't matter if the source of the pain is someone who is thirty-five or twelve years of age. No child deserves to be abused—by anyone.

At the conclusion of a professional training workshop that Fried conducted a number of years ago, a counselor shared her thoughts. The following is a paraphrase but accurate account of the conversation.

"In the beginning of this session, when you referred to bullying as a form of child abuse, I reacted negatively and thought you were exaggerating the situation. After being part of this training experience, and listening to the data, I think you should stop using the term *bullying* and use the term *abuse* instead. The term bullying is too benign. Too many people associate it with a childhood rite of passage and dismiss its effect. I am now convinced that too many children are in terrible pain and we have to use the strongest language possible to convey what is happening to them." The trauma that this thoughtful counselor referred to is affecting the culture of our educational system and bringing about a number of significant consequences that demand our concern.

TRUANCY AND DROP OUT PROBLEMS

According to the National Education Association, 160,000 children stay home from school every day. They are fearful about what is going to happen to them on the bus, on the playground, in the cafeteria, in the bathrooms, in the locker room, in the hallways, or in the classroom.

A truancy study looked at 25,000 eighth-grade students in some 1,000 schools over time to identify reasons that students drop out of school. Some factors were categorized as "push"—situations from within the school that pushed them out, such as feeling unsafe, feeling like they didn't belong, difficulties with other students, or being expelled—whereas others fell into the "pull" category—external factors that pulled them away from their educational path, such as marriage, pregnancy, having a job, or caring for a family member. The push factors appeared to be the most significant for predicting students' decisions to leave school. As a result, one of the suggestions for encouraging students to remain in school was to create a more positive and caring climate. We concur.

LEARNING ISSUES

Clearly, students who fear going to the bathroom and freeze at the thought of recess are going to have difficulty focusing on subject matter. A mind that is swirling with memories of past physical, verbal, emotional, sexual, and cyber bullying and terrified at the prospect of the next assault is not free to absorb complicated information. A student who is consumed with anxiety about what took place on the bus or what might happen in the cafeteria will have great difficulty concentrating on subject matter.

An example of this situation came to our attention at a private elementary school in Maryland. A parent spoke about her son's sudden drop in grades. Alan, who had always been an A student, was suddenly making C's and D's. It took a while to unravel the mystery, but what emerged was that the classroom teacher had established a rule that students who had not completed their homework assignments would not be permitted to participate in recess. Bingo! For Alan, who dreaded recess because of the bullying directed at him, this rule was his saving grace. He did as much homework as he could during the recess period, but it was never enough to keep him at his previous grade level. Avoiding recess trumped making A's for this student.

In light of the No Child Left Behind Act, which focuses on achievement accountability through test scores, a most interesting study has been released. As reported in the New York Times, Timothy Shriver and Roger

P. Weissberg conducted the largest-ever quantitative analysis, encompassing more than 300 research studies, to demonstrate the connection between the social and emotional needs of children and their academic performance.

The results show that when children are involved in effective social and emotional learning programs that help them make good choices, avoid bullying, and resist peer pressure to engage in destructive behaviors, they score at least 10 percentile points higher on achievement tests than students who do not participate in such programs. The article continues to report that compared with their counterparts outside of these programs, social and emotional learning students have significantly better attendance records, their classroom behavior is more constructive and less often disruptive, they like school more, and they have better grade point averages. They are also less likely to be suspended or otherwise disciplined. This landmark study validates what many professionals have always believed about the connection between bullying and academic achievement.

There is another aspect of academic success and bullying. Some students feel forced to choose between excelling in school and doing poorly to please their peers. Jealousy is frequently mentioned as a cause of bullying. This information comes from children who couldn't handle the harassment, from observant counselors and teachers, and from grateful parents who saw their children's grades improve when bullying prevention and intervention programs were initiated.

Far too often, the resistance to add antibullying programs in schools is based on the pressure of time limitations. Every precious minute of the school day is committed to increasing test scores. We sincerely hope that administrators and educators will come to appreciate that including social and emotional learning will not dilute academic achievement. To the contrary, it offers a strong case to combat truancy, to support academics, and to reduce dropout rates.

TEACHER SHORTAGES

Richard M. Ingersoll, Professor of Education and Sociology at the University of Pennsylvania, analyzed federal schools and staffing survey data from more than 50,000 teachers nationwide. Ingersoll reports that 33 percent of teachers leave the field after three years on the job and 43 percent leave within five years.

Suggestions for stemming the tide include increasing support for teachers, raising salaries, curbing student misbehavior, and giving faculty members more say in school decision making. Teachers also expressed concerns about school safety, student motivation, and discipline. Specifically, 25 percent of teachers said that student discipline drove them out, and 43 percent left because of inadequate support from school administration.

Teachers today are expected to be educators, social workers, parent surrogates, and law enforcement officers. Their dreams of educating young people about history, science, math, literature, language, and social studies are often deferred by the reality of the disruptive classroom. When we ask students how many of them want to be teachers when they reach adulthood, we are saddened by how few middle and senior high school students raise their hands and deeply concerned about the consequence for our society.

SUICIDE

In 2007, the Centers for Disease Control and Prevention reported that suicide was the third leading cause of death among youth and young adults. Though more females attempt suicide than males, males are much more likely to die from suicide.

Several studies have shown that gay, lesbian, and bisexual youths face an increased suicide risk. A survey published in the *American Journal of Public Health* found that gay high school students were about fourteen times more likely to attempt suicide than heterosexual students.

A number of parents have gone public and disclosed the devastating events of bullying that led to their children's suicides. In a number of cases, boys who were overweight were taunted, ostracized, and ridiculed beyond endurance. One father, on national television, spoke of what it was like to cut his firstborn son down from the limb of a tree, where he had hung himself in their backyard. The boy killed himself because, after a summer of dieting, he looked in the mirror and decided he wasn't thin enough to please his taunting classmates.

The word *bullycide* has now entered our language. Several recent books use this term in their title. Bullycide refers specifically to young people who commit suicide in connection with bullying experiences. One book, *Bullycide in America—Moms Speak Out about the Bullying/Suicide Connection,* chronicles the suicides of seven students who committed suicide because of bullying. Parents write about the loss of their beloved children because of bullying and document the details that led them to take their own lives. Each heartbreaking story provokes our outrage.

Fried trained one of the mothers, who was an eighth-grade science teacher at the time of her son's suicide, Debbie Johnston. Johnston channeled her anguish into an extraordinary campaign, involving busloads of young people traveling to Tallahassee, to persuade the Florida legislature to pass very strong antibullying legislation in 2008.

HEALTH ISSUES

The American Medical Association conducts yearly updates on significant health issues for media sources who write for TV, radio, magazines, journals, and the press. In August 2005, Fried was invited to make a presentation on bullying at such a briefing because of its health implications. Youth suicide is certainly a factor in peer abuse being identified as a health issue, but there are other reasons, too. Many mental health professionals report increasing connections between bullying and sleep disorders as well as eating disorder problems for children.

A study conducted at the University of Pittsburgh was the first research in the United States to measure how the hostility level of children affects physical changes, such as high blood pressure, body weight, unhealthy blood fats, and "insulin resistance"—ineffective processing of sugar. Children who scored at the top 25 percent on the hostility scale were at 50 percent greater risk for type 2 diabetes and heart disease.

There is a vicious cycle at play when hostile children compensate for their lack of successful social relationships by eating comfort foods. Their diet, laden with fats and sugar, causes weight gains and further increases the likelihood of bullying, states Karen Matthews, the study leader. Though hostility levels are about 30 percent genetic, parents can make a big impact by teaching youngsters how to manage anger and solve disputes without seething inside or erupting.

CRIME

More than thirty years ago, Leonard Eron, Ph.D., and his colleagues were one of the first groups of researchers in the country to look at the issue of bullying. Working with a school district in rural upper New York, they invited 875 third-grade students to indicate those classmates they considered to be bullies by putting a check mark beside their name. After collecting the bully nomination forms from the third graders, Eron and his team did extensive interviewing with family members, students, and teachers and stored those files for ten years.

A decade later, when the third graders had become seniors in high school, the researchers repeated the bully nomination process. Not surprisingly, they learned that most of the seniors who were marked as bullies by their peers were the same students identified as bullies when they were in the third grade.

When the original group of students was tracked, twenty years later, the research team discovered that one out of every four of the bullies, tagged by their eight- and nine-year-old peers, had a criminal record by the age of twenty-eight to thirty. The male bullies were at much greater risk of becoming abusive husbands, and the female bullies were more likely than their counterparts to have become abusive mothers. Other children have about a one-in-twenty chance of becoming adult criminals.

Research indicates that, in addition to criminal behavior, bullies are more likely to become involved in gangs and/or have employment difficulties, mental health problems, struggles with alcohol and substance abuse, and higher rates of divorce. The children identified as bullies in the third grade were more likely to become parents of children who were subsequently identified as bullies by their peers when they were in the third grade. Eron's study was the first to illustrate both the enduring nature of bullying behavior and the apparent intergenerational transmission of bullying behavior.

Support for these findings was demonstrated by Dan Olweus in a Norwegian study. He found that 60 percent of children identified as bullies between grades six and ten were cited for criminal behavior as adults, and 40 percent had three or more convictions.

Our traditional child protection system is not set up to protect children from abuse by other children. Adults, however, are protected from assault and harassment and can more readily use the judicial system to charge an attacker. Children, victims of the same assault by a peer, are left to the mercy of adults who may or may not intervene. Child abuse statutes in our fifty states specify the definition of child abuse as maltreatment perpetrated by an adult. Reports of children abused by other children are not customarily investigated by social service departments, unless they are sexual in nature.

There are legal aspects of bullying when it becomes extortion, theft, assault, battery, weapons possession, murder, arson, hate crime, hazing, sexual abuse, sexual harassment, rape, or a violation of civil rights. Those reports are handled by the juvenile justice system. Even though this process is quite intimidating, more parents are choosing to use the courts as a solution and are engaging lawyers to serve as legal advocates for their children's protection when schools are indifferent.

In one case, a school district was mandated to pay for the educational and counseling services for two children who had been forced to leave school because of harassment. A school district in Pennsylvania will pay $312,000 to settle a lawsuit filed by a gay teenager who alleged that officials did nothing to stop other students from tormenting him. He claimed he was pushed down stairs and subjected to other physical assaults as well as name-calling and obscene jokes. A jury awarded $250,000 to a Tonganoxie, Kansas, high school student on the plaintiff's claim that the Tonganoxie School District was deliberately indifferent to a same-sex student-on-student harassment in violation of Title IX of the Education Amendment Act of 1972.

SIBLING BULLYING

According to a study published in 2004, more than half of victims of bullying by siblings were also involved in bullying behavior at school compared to only 12.4 percent of those not victimized by siblings, indicating a strong link between intra-familial and extra-familial peer relationships. Children with poor sibling and peer relationships were at a highly increased risk for behavior problems.

David Finkelhor, a sociologist at the University of New Hampshire, reported that 35% of children had been hit or attacked by a sibling in the previous year. Vernon Wiehe, author and researcher, claims that 53 out of every 100 children abuse siblings. Renae D. Duncan studied the prevalence of bullying in 375 American children to determine the relationship between peer bullying and sibling bullying. Through a survey of male and female seventh and eighth grade students, she discovered that 28.2 percent acknowledged that they were bullies and 25.2 percent reported that they were victims. When they were asked about sibling interactions, 41.49 percent acknowledged that they were bullies and 29.94 percent reported that they were victims. Children who were both peer bullies and victims of peer bullying reported the highest frequency of sibling bullying and victimization.

Murray Strauss, an esteemed sociologist and researcher in the field of family violence, concluded that the sibling relationship was the most violent of human bonds—more than physical abuse of parents to children or husbands to spouses.

It is not surprising that a boy who is attacked on the school bus by a bully who forces his neck down between his legs goes home and takes his rage out on a younger brother by putting him in a stranglehold, a situation that came to light in a southern middle school. Reports from children across the country indicate that there is a strong connection between sibling bullying and peer bullying. Fried and a colleague, Lynne Lang, MHM, have given workshops on this subject at national and international conferences. Concerned responses from professionals and parents are convincing evidence that this issue bears more study.

Bullying deposits its toxic power and effects in the classroom, the school, the family, the community, the nation, and ultimately the world. Educators, counselors, parents, child advocates, and community activists are the gatekeepers of a civil society and role models for young people who will determine our destiny. There is much work to be done to make the world a kinder place for children.

Chapter 3

Back to Bullying Basics

The angel on one shoulder is telling me to do what is right and just.
The devil on the other says just go with the flow or you might be next.

—Clarisse, a student

DEFINING BULLYING

Based on a survey conducted by Fried and Fried, bullying behavior occurs when:

There Is Intent to Harm
The perpetrator finds pleasure in the taunting, which can be physical, verbal, emotional, sexual, and/or cyber bullying, and continues even when the target's distress is obvious.
There Is Intensity and Duration
The taunting continues over a long period of time, and the degree of taunting is damaging to the self-esteem of the target.
There Is Abuse of Power
The abuser maintains power over their target(s) because of age, strength, size, authority, and/or gender.
Bullying behavior is more likely to occur when:
The Target Is Vulnerable
The target is more sensitive to teasing, cannot adequately defend him/herself, and has physical or psychological qualities that make him or her more prone to vulnerability.

19

The Target Is Unsupported
The target feels isolated and exposed. The target is often afraid to report the
  abuse for fear of retaliation.
The Target Experiences Significant Consequences
The damage to self-concept is long lasting and the target responds to the
  abuse with either withdrawal or aggression, which rewards the bully.

The first three elements focus on the status of the bully. The last three elements focus on the status of the target. Because most bullying is unobserved
by adults, we believe that changes in the behavior of the target might be
noticed before indications are detected in the behavior of the bully.

EXTENT OF BULLYING

"Bullying Behaviors Among U.S. Youth: Prevalence and Association with
Psychosocial Adjustment" was published in the Journal of the American
Medical Association in 2001 and is widely quoted as a major assessment of
the extent of bullying in the United States. A representative sample of 15,686
students in grades six through ten in public and private schools throughout
the United States completed a self-reporting survey sponsored by the World
Health Organization. According to the report, a total of 29.9 percent of the
sample reported moderate or frequent involvement in bullying: as a bully
(13.0 percent), one who was bullied (10.6 percent), or both (6.3 percent).

Males were more likely than females to be both perpetrators and targets of
bullying. The frequency of bullying was higher among sixth- through eighth-
grade students than among ninth- and tenth-grade students. The study found
that both bullies and those bullied demonstrate poorer psychosocial functioning than their noninvolved peers. As to the prevalence of bullying, the report
extrapolated that 5,736,417 youth are involved in some type of moderate or
frequent bullying. The report concludes that "The prevalence of bullying
among U.S. youth is substantial," and "the issue of bullying merits serious
attention, both for future research and preventive intervention."

It is significant to note that the report did not include data from elementary
school students. We feel strongly that prevention strategies should begin
in the primary grades, before students become indoctrinated in the middle
school culture.

A more recent estimate of the extent of bullying comes from Bully Police
USA. Based on 2000 census figures and a Norwegian study of Dan Olweus,
an internationally respected researcher, there are 8,824,833 students involved
as bullies, targets, and bully/targets.

One of the most significant aspects of these studies was retrieving information from students who defined themselves as both bullies and being bullied. Frans de Waal, a primatologist at Emory University, thinks we should study the characteristics of the bully and the scapegoat/target simultaneously. In primate groups, he observed a pattern of interaction whereby those at the top of the hierarchy harass subordinates simply because they can.

At the same time, low-ranking members of the hierarchy are selected by the group to become the resident scapegoat. This seemingly innate dance serves a useful purpose for the group. It unites them against a common enemy and serves as a bonding experience. Researchers who have studied family systems have come to similar conclusions about the scapegoating syndrome in families. The most powerful person in the system will begin to target a weaker member and the other family members will join in the game. This gives other weak members a way to solidify their own uncertain position within the family system. Peer bullying frequently follows a similar pattern. Weak students join forces with bullies to acquire status they were previously denied.

BULLYING AS A SOCIETAL CONCERN

The multiple shooting of twelve students and a teacher at Columbine High School by Eric Harris and Dylan Klebold in Littleton, Colorado, April 20, 1999, was the turning point of the bullying issue in the United States. In addition to the twelve students who died, twenty-three were injured, several critically, from which they will never fully recover.

First reports from the media who interviewed escaping students produced implications that bullying led to the tragic shootings. Once the visual images of students jumping out of windows, children running and crying, armed police officers, sirens, ambulances become imprinted on the national psyche and was attached to the bullying, there was an eruption of interest in the topic. Prior to that traged, there were relatively few people who were researching, thinking, and concerned about bullying. The fact that the Columbine tragedy occurred in an affluent, mostly white suburban school shattered the illusion of immunity from school violence that many students and parents had previously held. This combination of factors led to an unprecedented focus on the cruelty of children to each other.

A recent book, *Columbine,* by David Cullen, debunks the theory that Harris and Klebold became killers because of bullying. Cullen's thoughtful research indicates that Eric Harris was a brilliant but psychopathic youg man who was

obsessed with blowing up his high school and found an initially reluctant
partner in Dylan Klebold, a depressed fellow student. Though Klebold had
known rejection in his school experiences, the carnage he participated in cannot be directly traced to traumatizing bullying at Columbine High School.

Assumptions were made at the time based on quotes from a very small
number of the 2,000 students under inordinate stress. Bullying was a problem
at Columbine, as it was and is at schools all over the country, but because of a
frenzy to come up with a reason for such a shocking event, those observations
became cemented in public opinion. Other beliefs that have been devoutly
held are also laid open for scrutiny in *Columbine.*

Ten years later we have the opportunity to learn new information about
what really happened. What cannot be denied is that the cause and effect
assumptions about bullying led to intense national and international concern.
The compelling interest led to tremendous exposure of bullying issues on
television, newspapers, radio, and magazines. Surveys, research, programs
and an abundance of materials resulted.

TERMINOLOGY

Abuse/Bullying

As expressed in the previous chapter, we will use the term abuse and bullying
synonymously. An interesting side-note is that current reports indicate that
899,000 reports of child abuse are confirmed annually. In response to that
appalling data, our society has created multiple resources and responses—
including child abuse investigation services, national data collection, foster
care and adoption programs, respite care, termination of parental rights, per-
manency planning, case management, counseling, prevention services, and so
on—costing billions of dollars.

For bullying, or peer abuse, which is estimated at between 5,000,000 and
8,000,000 cases annually, there is no national strategy in place. As of this
writing 38 states have passed anti-bullying legislation but there are great
variations in the bills and many mandates provide no monies or accountability to ensure enforcement of the legislative elements.

Teasing vs. Bullying

Many people believe that teasing and bullying are synonymous, but most
students hold to the opinion that not all teasing is bullying. Teasing is not bullying when there is mutual give and take, sometimes affectionate, sometimes
humorous, a bantering style of communication where there is equal power. It

can also be part of the student culture where children chide and corral each other to stay in touch with the expectations of their peers. Many professionals believe that teasing can be helpful and lead to more intimacy.

Bullying on the other hand, can be described as a situation where one person does all the giving and the other does all the taking. There is no fun for the person on the receiving end and, as one bright student from Clay Center, Kansas, suggested, "Teasing is when two people are laughing, bullying is when only one person is laughing."

Bullies

There are some who have suggested that we should not label children as bullies, that we should talk about children who engage in bullying behaviors lest we stereotype a child who is struggling to find a sense of personal power in a powerless arena. There are some who say that almost every child has been a bully and/or been bullied and the roles are quite interchangeable. To that point, Dorothy Espelage, Ph.D., of the University of Illinois at Urbana-Champaign says that nearly 80 to 90 percent of adolescents report some form of victimization from a bully at school, and kids who bully a lot also say they've been victimized. Dr. Espelage believes that we should describe bullying as a continuum of behaviors rather than label any child a bully, nonbully, or victim.

We concur with those observations. We have decided to use the term *bully* with misgivings, precisely because of the labeling issue. We recognize that many bullies move back and forth in the role of targets and bullies and are often referred to in the literature as bully/victims. We are using this terminology as a kind of communication shorthand, and it is very important to us that our readers know our concern is for all children. We believe that every child deserves to be seen as a whole child who behaves in a strategic way toward some end. As one parent pleaded so convincingly: "My child has been involved in bullying behavior on occasion, but if you knew my child, you would never think of him as a bully!"

Targets

SuEllen Fried and her daughter, Paula Fried, used the term *victim* in their first book, *Bullies & Victims—Helping Your Child through the Schoolyard Battlefield,* published in 1996. After working with thousands of students and educators, it became clear that the term *victim* implies helplessness and excludes the power of hopefulness. The Frieds' second book was titled *Bullies, Targets & Witnesses—Helping Children Break the Pain Chain.*

Thus, we have chosen to use the term target because it implies that you may be the object of an attack, but the assault may not be successful. The arrow, so to speak, may completely miss the intended target or, even if it manages to arrive, can be deflected. There are many children who learn how to avoid being victimized by their peers.

Students definitely prefer the word target, although one earnest student suggested that we should have called our book Bullies & Ducks. She explained that she had a teacher who told the class: "If you walk like a duck, and you talk like a duck, and you act like a duck, you're going to be a duck!" The student then observed that students who "walk like targets, talk like targets, and act like targets are going to be targets!"

Witnesses

Regarding children who observe bullying, we are committed to the term witness. Much of the bullying literature uses the term bystander. We believe this word is too passive and lacks the mobilizing energy that is required of peers to become actively engaged. When asked to define a witness, many students have watched the numerous law programs on TV and are quick to describe a witness as "someone who sees what happens and has to tell the truth." This definition more aptly prescribes one of the actions we heartily endorse for students—to report bullying situations to an adult.

While this may seem to be an obvious reaction, for many children it is fraught with risk. They have concerns about being labeled a "snitch" or "tattletale." In some communities and cultures there is a deeply held code to withhold personal knowledge from authorities. An often used phrase is, "Snitches get stitches and end up in ditches."

Even teachers who are conscientious about bullying issues don't realize how much abuse occurs when they are not present or aware of the behavior. A study by Wendy Craig from Queen's University and Debra Pepler from York University determined that 71 percent of teachers say they almost always intervene in bullying, whereas students say that teachers intervene only 25 percent of the time. Pepler and Craig's observations indicate that teachers intervene in 14 percent of classroom episodes and in only 4 percent of playground episodes of bullying.

We believe this discrepancy should not assume that teachers don't care; it is that they aren't there. Bullies can be Machiavellian in their plots to thwart detection. There are infinite opportunities for students to bully their peers when adults are not around or their backs are turned. The possibilities for abuse on buses and playgrounds and in bathrooms, cafeterias, locker rooms, hallways, and classrooms are infinite.

We are convinced that one of the most hopeful strategies for reducing bullying is to engage witnesses as key players. They are present, they are fully aware of the depth and breadth of the abuse, and they can be provided with skills to use a number of options for prevention and intervention.

While writing this book, Fried attended the sorrowful funeral of a beloved seventeen-year-old student, Bryan Barrow, who died in an automobile accident. At a celebration of his life service, a number of his friends spoke about him, and one of them, Bill, described an unforgettable moment. He recalled an incident concerning a girl in their class who had no eyebrows. A boy started making fun of her and Bryan said to him, "Why would you say something like that to a girl who is working so hard to stay confident about herself?"

The bully backed off immediately. Bill was deeply impressed with Bryan's courage and vowed to take similar action the next time he witnessed an act of cruelty. At the conclusion of the service, everyone was asked to take away one quality of Bryan's they would add to their lives as a way of keeping his spirit alive. Hundreds of students left that service with "courage" on their minds and in their hearts. They will be witnesses who make a difference.

ORIGINS OF BULLYING

Family Issues

Bullying is a learned behavior, acquired primarily from family members and/or friends. There is almost universal agreement that bullies generally become bullies through their life experiences. Bullies are more likely to have been abused themselves and/or have witnessed their fathers physically abusing their mothers. Bullies might have been abused by their siblings. When they are unprotected at home, students often use classmates as an outlet for their anger.

Defense Strategy

Many bullies started out as targets and learned that their best defense was being aggressive. A compelling example came from Mitch who tried every response possible to avoid fighting back. He tried ignoring the bully, using his words, reporting the situation to adults, hiding from the bully, making a joke, but nothing stopped the bully from tormenting him—day after day after day. His father kept insisting that the only way to handle such a tyrant was to settle it with his fists. Mitch had no desire to start a fight with Jesse, but after months of relentless bullying, he punched the bully in the face. To his great surprise, the bullying stopped. Mitch didn't want to solve his problem that way. He didn't want to become a bully. But in the end, for him it was the only method that worked.

Inborn Traits

We must acknowledge that there are children who are more likely to become bullies because of inborn traits, such as those who were crack babies, who suffered from fetal alcohol syndrome, and some children with attention deficit disorder (ADD) or attention deficit hyperactivity disorder (ADHD) whose disruptive behavior patterns may have a biological basis.

In the past several years, a mounting number of children who have been diagnosed with Asperger's syndrome, a mild form of autism, are entering the school system. Psychiatrist Leo Kanner was the first person to apply the term autism to children who were socially withdrawn, preoccupied with routine, and had difficulty with language yet often possessed a level of intelligence that ruled out mental retardation. The following year, in 1944, Hans Asperger applied the term to children who were socially awkward and consumed with bizarre obsessions, yet highly verbal and very bright. These children have shown up as targets and occasionally bullies because of social-skill issues.

Media Influence

A large body of research data has confirmed the correlation between TV watching and aggressive behavior. One study followed 707 children in upstate New York for seventeen years. The researchers documented the viewing habits of the students beginning in 1983 when they were fourteen years old, and again, eight years later, when they were well into adulthood.

Teens who watched three or more hours of TV a day were five times more likely to commit aggressive acts in the next several years as those who watched less than one hour a day. Among those who watched TV less than one hour a day in 1983, fewer than 6 percent were found to have committed an aggressive act in the next eight years, compared with 22.5 percent of those who watched one to three hours, and 28.8 percent of those who watched more than three hours daily. Acts considered aggressive were assaults resulting in injury, threats of violence, robberies, and use of a weapon in a crime.

Researchers have determined that there is an even stronger relationship between playing violent computer games and aggressive behavior. In one study, subjects were asked to play one of two video games: Mist, an analytic virtual computer game or Wolfenstein, a violent video game where the object is to track down and brutally kill their enemies. After playing the video game, subjects were observed in a laboratory with a peer. Subjects who had played Wolfenstein were consistently more aggressive toward the peer in the laboratory situation.

Other violent video games, such as Grand Theft Auto, have been exposed and deservedly condemned. But then there are those, including our own family members, who point out the value of analytic video games that promote complex thinking and thoughtful responses to solve problems. There are many such games that motivate the player to explore optional solutions to complicated problems. These games, which require work and patience to gather information, stimulate the imagination, and improve skills to create inventive solutions, need to be appreciated.

The American Medical Association contends that media violence causes an increase in mean-spirited, aggressive behavior; causes increased levels of fearfulness, mistrust, and self-protective behavior toward others; contributes to desensitization and callousness to the effects of violence and suffering of others; provides justification for resorting to violence when children think they are right; and fosters a culture in which disrespectful behavior becomes a legitimate way for people to treat each other.

Commonsense Media, a nonpartisan watchdog group, reports that children spend an average of 30 hours a week in school while spending nearly 45 hours a week immersed in media—almost three times the amount of time they spend with their parents.

PROFILES OF BULLIES

Several researchers have investigated the cognitive processes or thinking patterns of bullies. Psychologists Kenneth Dodge, Ph.D., and John Coie, Ph.D., have described two different styles of aggression in their research with children: reactive and proactive.

Reactive bullies are aggressive children with poor impulse control who react to an accidental bump as an act of provocation. These children see the world though a paranoid lens, feel constantly threatened, and thus believe that their aggressive response is justified. An accidental brush against such a child's arm can be interpreted as a direct assault. These children do not see themselves as bullies but as protectors of their space. In their minds it is the other child who is the troublemaker. These thinking patterns are well in place by the age of seven or eight.

Proactive bullies, on the other hand, are more calculating about initiating hurtful acts. They behave in a nonemotional, controlled, deliberate manner. They are selective about their targets and look for satisfaction and rewards in their choosing. The aggression is delivered with the hope of achieving some goal that comes from within the aggressive child, like coercion or domination, rather than in response to some external threat.

Robert Selman, Ph.D., has examined another aspect of the thinking patterns of bullies. He focuses on the immaturity of bullies' cognitive style, describing it as unilateral in nature. These children think in terms of simple one-way directives and commands to others—for example, "Give that to me." They lack the more mature form of thinking that allows for a reciprocal exchange of ideas and collaboration that enable people to effectively resolve differences with each other. Selman and his colleagues suggest that this type of bully has limited skills to mange relationship conflicts and this, in turn, leads to anger and aggression.

The elitist bully is a third kind of bully that we have observed. This is the bully who is very attractive, or is an outstanding athlete, or has acquired social status because of his or her parents' financial, corporate, or political position. Not all children become corrupted by their elitism but a significant number succumb to the power given them and use it to torment those they feel are inferior. We have heard countless stories of "jocks," athletes who take advantage of their fame to ridicule and humiliate other students. Often they are even bold enough to do it in the presence of coaches and other faculty members, knowing they will never be admonished. School rules, which all other students are expected to follow, are not applied to them.

A particular case in point is a young female student, Veronica, at a private school who was extremely malicious and verbally hurtful to other students, especially to girls. A fellow classmate commented, "She lives in a palace, she's treated like a princess, and she thinks she is more important than other people." One of the mothers consistently complained to the principal, who appeared to be sympathetic to the specific incidents that were described. As time went on, and Veronica's behavior never changed, the mother sought out other parents to see if they were mindful of the problem. They added their tales of abuse regarding their targeted daughters, but all concluded that because her family had made considerable contributions to the building fund, the offender would never be reprimanded.

However, many children of high-profile, extremely successful parents are class leaders, are models of considerate behavior, and have learned at an early age to become responsible citizens with a commitment to a greater good.

PROFILES OF TARGETS

When students are asked why some of their peers become targets, they usually reply: "Because they are different." However, the list of differences they identify is almost endless—everything from weight and height to hair color and skin color to lack of agility or too much ability. By the time we vet the list, everyone in the class fits into at least one of the categories, so being different cannot be a legitimate reason.

Students become targets because a bully thinks it's cool to be cruel and gets pleasure out of another person's pain. Some students do seem to send a message that attracts bullies. It can be in their vulnerable body language, their obvious distress, the way they send some kind of a signal to bullies on alert.

Gary Ladd, Ph.D., a psychologist, conducted a study and discovered that bullies engage in a "shopping" process to find students who will become their preferred targets. Ladd suggests that bullies do not pick on others at random, but use a calculating strategy to narrow their selection. While over half of the students in his study reported being victimized at least once a year, and about 22 percent of the students reported being victimized frequently at the beginning of the school year, by the end of the year only 8 percent of students reported being regularly subjected to a bully's attacks.

Ladd believes that some targets are more likely to reward their bullies—tangibly by giving up their lunch money, for example, or intangibly by showing distress and giving the bully a sense of power. These targets are also less likely to retaliate or cause the bully to be punished.

We have identified these behaviors as the Cry, Comply, Deny, Fly Off the Handle syndrome.

Cry—Targets who cry make bullies feel very powerful. While crying may be a natural, legitimate response, postponing tears can be very helpful.

Comply—Targets who willingly relinquish their homework, their lunch money, their lunch, or the ball they are playing with will find the bully coming back to them over an over again because they offer no resistance.

Deny—Targets who are easily intimidated and pose no threat of reporting their tormentor are more likely to be selected. Even when asked, some targets will firmly deny the identity of their abuser, out of fear of retaliation.

Fly Off the Handle—Targets can be manipulated by bullies to explode on cue, just as an adult enters the scene. The target is the one that gets in trouble, which gives the bully enormous satisfaction.

Researchers have identified two types of targets. Olweus describes them as passive (anxious and insecure) and provocative (hot-tempered and restless). David Perry, Ph.D., describes them as low aggressive and high aggressive.

Passive targets appear to do nothing to invite the bully's aggression, and also do not attempt to defend themselves when attacked. They are usually soft-spoken, shy, and lack self-confidence.

Provocative targets create tension by irritating and annoying others and are more likely to fight back when attacked. Provocative targets may have ADHD, Asperger's syndrome, or learning disabilities that prevent them from picking up on social cues other children intuitively understand. These children can irritate others without even realizing it.

There are some targets who prefer negative attention to no attention at all. They are so starved for recognition, so unwilling to be a cipher, that they tolerate abuse as an affirmation of their existence. We believe, however, that most targets would choose not to be taunted or excluded and would happily trade places with classmates who manage to escape the anxiety and embarrassment that plague their lives. Targets need to realize that their "flaw" is not the cause of their torment. We need to help them understand that the problem lies with the bully, not with them. At the same time, we must assist them to understand how their behavior unwittingly contributes to their vulnerability to bullying.

PROFILES OF WITNESSES

What about those children who witness cruelty and feel helpless to alter the situation? If you can't protect others, can you ensure safety for yourself? What are the lifelong effects of guilt brought about by not speaking up? Again, there are many areas of this issue that have not been fully explored.

Numerous parents have described childhood situations in which they were acutely aware of a classmate's raw wounds and did nothing to intervene. Some have even shared poignant stories of having joined the group assault for self-protection. As they watch their children endure the indignities of others, they are racked by painful memories of their own sins of omission and commission.

Nedra, a soft-spoken conference participant from the Midwest, told the story of attending a rural school where most of the children rode the bus. One little girl became the scapegoat for all the other bus riders, who refused to have any contact with her. This woman reported the only fault she could remember this girl possessed was to have lived the farthest away. For that reason alone, other children decided to ostracize her. After a while it became habitual, and no one wanted to be the first to contradict the school-bus culture.

Years later, Nedra became a psychiatric nurse. On her first day of employment at the hospital where she had been assigned, a patient approached her. The patient stared at her and said, "Do you remember me"? The nurse immediately recognized the withdrawn woman as the girl who had been ignored all those early years. The nurse replied, "Yes, I do." The patient looked her directly in the eye and said, "I just want you to see where you are and where I am."

These memories haunt the souls of men and women who participated, sometimes inadvertently, in childhood acts of cruelty. They agonize as they try to reconcile the person they are now with the wounds they caused others in the past. We heard the story of a man who chose not to attend his high school reunion but sent a videotape instead. In the tape he expressed shame and remorse for the hurtful ways he had treated his classmates when he was young. There is a good chance, however, that the people he hurt so badly did not attend the reunion, either. Adults who live with unresolved pain from their childhood frequently avoid contact with any reminders of their painful past.

Sometimes you can make amends. Singer, songwriter, and minister Lee Domann composed a poignant song called "Howard Gray" about his role in taunting a seventh-grade classmate whose real name was Howard Ray, Jr. A Kansas native who now resides in Nashville, Tennessee, Domann turned the song into an education video and is committed to its distribution as an instrument to promote tolerance and acceptance, especially between children. Ray and Domann reconnected many years later, after Ray had heard the song and decided to forgive his former tormentor.

Sometimes you cannot make amends, but you can atone. Brandi Guardino, a woman who has become a dedicated advocate of bullying prevention, shared the following story on a radio interview. When she was in sixth grade, a girl in her class who was quite large for her age, started developing more quickly than the other girls. A popular saying at that time was "Where's the beef?", so the kids started calling her "Beefer." One day a substitute teacher was calling the roll and when she came to the name of the targeted girl, the students told the teacher her name was Beefer, so for the next three days the substitute teacher called the girl Beefer. The target was too embarrassed to ask the teacher to call her by her real name.

To add to her humiliation, every day in gym class a group of girls would grab her towel when she stepped out of the shower. She would cower in the corner to hide her body and cried as she pulled on her wet clothes, only to be ridiculed because of the way her clothing clung to her skin.

Years later, Brandi was working for a psychiatrist and was asked to file the chart of a deceased female patient who had committed suicide. Because they were the same age, the doctor asked if she knew the former client. She did not recognize the client's name, but when she reviewed the client's history, she realized that the young woman was Beefer.

Brandi is now determined to do whatever she can to prevent this situation from being repeated with another child. While she did not participate in the devastating activities, she feels deep remorse for not making some effort to support the reviled young girl.

One result is that, as president of the Catawba County Medical Society Alliance in North Carolina, she made bullying prevention a priority project for her group. Fried was asked to conduct the BullySafeUSA Training Institute in the North Carolina community for twenty-two school counselors who will now present that program to thousands of students in their local schools. Sometimes there is nothing you can do to erase the sins of the past, but you can use your energy to shape the future.

Fried believes that witnesses react to the bullying they observe in a variety of ways. Their responses fall into several categories.

Blockers—Withdraw from the action and build a wall around their feelings.
Self-protectors—Focus on how to avoid bullying attacks, at all costs.
Judgers—Become annoyed because targets won't defend themselves.
Voyeurs—Receive some sadistic pleasure out of viewing someone else's anguish.
Accomplices—Directly or indirectly support bullies and give them power.
Empathizers—Feel concern for the targets but lack confidence to intervene.
Champions—Take some action to relieve the target's pain.

When you share these categories with your students, it is important to allow them to recognize their reactions without being critical of their reflections. By identifying their responses to uncomfortable situations, young people can begin to find an action at their comfort level. With intent and practice, they could become champions instead of passive bystanders.

Many adults behave in similar fashion. The infamous Kitty Genovese murder in New York City many years ago was the shameful example of dozens of eye-witnesses to a stabbing that was taking place on the sidewalk in front of a large apartment building. The weather was warm, windows were open, and the residents heard Kitty's screams for help as they watched in horror. Not one witness came to her rescue or even called the police. Everyone assumed that somebody else would take action, so nobody took responsibility.

Law enforcement officers struggling with increasing violence in their cities are deeply frustrated by the unwillingness of community members to come forward with information about known perpetrators. This resistance is hampering efforts to keep serial criminals off the streets. A change in attitude in our society is long overdue.

Involving adults is critical to preventing abuse—and tragedies. A three-year partnership between the U.S. Department of Education and the U.S. Secret Service resulted in a joint report, the Safe School Initiative. One of the most critical findings was that before more than 75 percent of the incidents, at least one person knew about the attacker's idea or plan to attack. Most attackers also engaged in some behavior that caused others concern or indicated a need for help. In virtually all the cases where someone knew of the plan, the person with advance notice was a peer—a friend, a schoolmate, or sibling. In only two cases did an adult know of the idea or plan.

On an encouraging note, administrators are pointing out that students are much more likely to report rumors or threats of violence than they were in years past. In fact, a survey released in the publication *Save Our Kids* indicates that 81 percent of teens state they are more willing, in the aftermath of Columbine, to report students who threaten their safety. Young people are learning that silence hurts and they can save lives when they speak up. A number of tragedies have been averted, but without the headlines that shootings attract.

In our purpose to illuminate the definitions and terminology of bullying behavior and the profiles of bullies, targets, and witnesses, we feel compelled to restate that first and foremost we are holding all children in our embrace. Our shorthand labels are meant to be helpful in grasping the idiosyncrasies of bullying, not to alienate our concern even for young people who are practicing cruelty.

If bullying is a learned behavior, who taught the bullies how to inflict pain? Why do some children find pleasure in the torment of others? If they are too wounded before we discover them, can we make sure that they have access to therapeutic interventions before we expel them from our view?

How can we make sure that every child is protected from the onslaught of brutality, humiliation, and isolation? How can we reassure the ridiculed that they are of value? How can we support them to convert their youthful suffering to become adults who are social healers and advocates for kindness?

As we continue analyzing the seemingly infinite elements of our subject, let us never forget we are discussing the fate of those who were innocents, only a short time ago.

Chapter 4

How Can I Hurt Thee? Let Me Count The Ways

When I see bullying I feel really bad for the person that is being picked on and harassed, but then again, I feel good because it is not me being bullied.

—Mandy, a student

Physical, Verbal, Emotional, Sexual, and Cyber Bullying

BULLYING TRENDS

Bullying today is more complex, more lethal, and considerably different in many ways from bullying in the past. Bullying then was typically synonymous with physical abuse, and even the physical abuse rarely resulted in death. The legendary phrase, "Sticks and stones can break my bones, but words can never hurt me," obscured our willingness to take the verbal assaults that children experienced seriously. Emotional bullying, with its invisible fingerprints, was rarely identified, and sexual bullying with its elements of sexual curiosity and teen angst was ever present, but not as devastating as it has become today. Cyber bullying, the use of various forms of electronic technology to cause pain, really didn't emerge until the twenty-first century but has quickly taken its place as a viral form of hurtfulness.

Even our definition of physical bullying requires expansion. Added to yesterday's choking, kicking, and fisticuffs, which produced bruises, welts,

35

and broken limbs, are today's stabbings, shootings, and pipe bombs, which produce gaping wounds, paralysis, lifelong injuries, and death. This chapter will explore these various types of bullying in their current form. The data we will share is the result of conversations with over 85,000 students in public, private, parochial, urban, rural, and suburban schools all across the country; discussions with tens of thousands educators and parents; as well as significant research.

Physical Bullying

Students define physical bullying as punching, shoving, choking, tripping, poking, stabbing, spitting, beating up, kicking, throwing an object at someone, pushing someone into a locker, taking someone's lunch money, giving someone a black eye, tearing someone's clothes, head butting, shooting, swirlies, stabbing, noogies, nipple twisting, jabbing, throwing someone in the trash can, stepping on someone's toes, urinating on someone, and wrestling holds. One student even reported being held down while cigarette smoke was blown into her mouth until she vomited.

Girls are more likely to slap, pull hair, scratch, pinch, dig their fingernails into someone, or bite. Boys are more likely to punch, choke, kick, throw objects, and use weapons. Boys have mentioned that girls take advantage of their gender, knowing that they can slap, scratch, or pinch with impunity, as it is considered ungentlemanly for the males to retaliate against a female peer. Physical contact of any kind that is hurtful or harmful is a form of physical abuse. Students find it quite easy to give examples.

"This boy would always come up from behind me and pull on my bookbag until I lost my balance. Once he did it while I was walking up the stairs and I fell down six or seven stairs onto the concrete landing. All the other students just walked on by and a lot of them laughed."

"I was standing in line in the cafeteria and the girl behind me suddenly attacked me with a broken mirror she had in her purse. She slashed my shoulder and I was bleeding all over my clothes. I was terrified. They took me to the hospital and my attacker was expelled. To this day, I still don't know why she decided to cut on me."

Cutting brings up the subject of self-mutilation. The act of cutting oneself is also referred to as self-injury or nonsuicidal self-injury. Other forms of self-injury include skin picking, biting, and burning, but cutting is the most frequent form. These acts of self destruction are much too common among teenage girls.

Researchers who are trying to understand the underlying reasons for such injurious behavior point to relief of tension, self-punishment, numbness, and the need to feel in control and to create visible and treatable wounds. It is certainly an unhealthy coping mechanism for young people who are dealing with anxiety and depression. Destructive behavior—whether it comes from others, or whether it comes from within, requires intervention.

Though school violence is decreasing in some communities, we've heard countless stories about bloody beatings, fistfights between girls, and the increased use of weapons. Some disturbing trends include the younger age of offending students, the greater availability of guns, and female involvement in physical aggression. In the last months of 2008 there were two reports of female on female violence that made national headlines—one involving a shooting, the other a stabbing.

In April 2002 in Chicago, nearly two dozen children ages ten to fourteen were arrested on charges of mob action against students from a nearby school. Their weapons were baseball bats and planks of wood. Their victims were eighteen students who were treated for cuts and bruises at hospitals. The assault occurred on the school playground before school began. Although these students used baseball bats and wood planks, a growing number have used guns. According to the World Health Organization, "In one year, firearms killed zero children in Japan, 19 in Great Britain, 57 in Germany, 109 in France, 153 in Canada and 5,285 in the United States." Metal detectors in our schools would have been unthinkable a few decades ago.

Whenever we work with police officers, or peace officers as they are called in some places, they remind us that laws designed to protect adults from physical assault are invisible with respect to children. How can we watch all the footage of playground battles aired on national TV shows, children ganging up and kicking a contorted classmate, videotapes of youngsters pummeling a helpless student, and not make the connection that this is criminal behavior? How can we criminalize adult victimization and then dismiss it as a "rite of passage" when the victim is a student?

Verbal Bullying

Defining verbal abuse also obliges us to broaden our long held ideas. Today's children are exposed to an unconscionable lack of civility. Curse words that were culturally verboten yesterday are in common usage today. A survey conducted by a nonprofit research group, Public Agenda, reported that 79 percent of the adults interviewed said that a lack of respect and courtesy in American society is a serious problem and more than a third admitted that they use foul language in public.

Lilia Cortina and Vicki Magley, reporting the results of research at a meeting of the APA, found that "in your face" rudeness is rampant in the U.S. workplace.

Their study indicated that 71 percent of 1,100 workers surveyed said they had experienced put-downs or condescending and outright rude behavior on the job. As encounters with uncivil behavior rose, so did symptoms of anxiety and depression. Those who were passive and did nothing about their maltreatment had the worst mental health. These findings are relevant to bullying issues—for educators and students.

"Trash talk" is currently accepted as the norm. Models for young people in sports, entertainment, and politics have broken all the boundaries of refined behavior. People who engage in questionable ethics are rewarded with fame, power, and money. No wonder, then, that children imitate our current icons and bring to the playground a kind of social warfare that would have been unthinkable forty or fifty years ago. Young people who have not developed the maturity to sort out fantasy and reality, short-term and long-term consequences, and power and control, are parading in an adult world without the inner character to make good choices.

Verbal bullying can be name-calling, put-downs, threatening, cursing, swearing, yelling, making up stories, gossiping, spreading rumors, talking about someone's mother or another family member, telling "mama" jokes, making fun of someone's physical characteristics, imitating a lisp or a stutter, screaming, being sarcastic, ridiculing, making up a derogatory song, daring someone, or whispering about someone as they approach. Any use of language or words to hurt someone would qualify as verbal bullying.

Every child can complete the expression that begins with "Sticks and stones." This sentence has been handed down for four or five generations and it isn't true. In *Bullies & Victims,* Fried asked students to change the phrase to "Sticks and stones can break your bones, but words can break your heart." Students report that a broken bone can heal in a matter of weeks, perhaps a few months, or sometimes even a year but a broken heart may never heal. Here are two stories shared by students.

"There was this one student who wouldn't ever say my first name, but would always call me 'Jew girl'. Then he would go on to say that 'Your people cause all of the wars.' I'm not even Jewish, but my last name could be!"

"My ears stuck out and all the kids started calling me 'Dumbo'. They never let up. I got so sick of it, I begged and pleaded with my parents to let me have surgery to make my ears smaller. They finally agreed, but I will never forget how miserable I was."

Many students have shared their pain about being called names because of their race, their culture, their size, their height, or a perceived shortcoming of some kind. Frequently, students will talk about how much it hurts to have someone say something about their mother. There is a collection of "mama" jokes that has traveled all across the country, such as "Your mother is so fat that she has to use the highway for a sidewalk." Some students say it doesn't bother them because they know kids are just repeating jokes, but other students confess that it really gets to them to have someone say something nasty about their mother, regardless of the origin.

During a discussion with a very bright fifth-grade class, a girl brought up the subject of daring someone to do something that can be dangerous. When asked if she had a particular situation in mind, she shared a family story.

When her father and his brother were in their teens, her uncle dared her father to jump into a river that was swollen with rushing water. To prove that he was not a coward, her father jumped in and immediately found himself unable to swim against the water's force. As he was dragged downstream, his brother became terrified and ran for help. Her father survived two miles in treacherous waters before he was rescued. He recounted the story to impress upon his children how important it is not to feel challenged by a dare that puts you at risk. In our community there have been several fatal automobile accidents related to "hill jumping," and there was speculation that some of those fatalities had resulted from dares.

On the subject of rumors, a middle school girl raised her hand one time to ask about "spreading the truth." When asked to elaborate, she said: "What if you confide a secret to a friend and ask her not to tell anyone and then she betrays you and tells everyone in the class what you told her? Does that count as verbal bullying?" Students, when asked, will always confirm that they consider betrayal of a secret a form of verbal bullying.

One student raised the question, if the secret is a confession of being abused, shouldn't you tell someone? That was an important difference to make, but everyone agreed that the best procedure would be to tell a counselor or the principal but certainly not other classmates.

An adult who was present during a discussion of "spreading the truth" related a personal story after the class left. When she was in the third grade, a friend invited her to her very first sleepover. She had never slept at someone else's home, and she was quite excited about the prospect. She recalled the thrill of packing her suitcase with her pajamas, toothbrush, and clean clothing. She knew she was excited but didn't realize that she was nervous. That night, for the first time, she wet the bed. She was horribly embarrassed, but the worst was yet to come. When she and her hostess returned to school, the hostess told everyone about her accident. As she said: "My friend didn't make up a story about me, she didn't spread a rumor about me, all she did was tell the truth, but no one ever invited me to spend the night with them during all my years at school."

Emotional Bullying

Emotional bullying includes psychological and nonverbal bullying. Physical, verbal, sexual, and cyber bullying have emotional/psychological consequences, as well, but our definition of emotional bullying has a distinct set of behaviors. We define emotional bullying as a type of abuse in which there is no physical contact and no words are exchanged. There are two categories of emotional bullying: nonverbal and psychological.

Nonverbal emotional bullying is pointing, staring, mugging, laughing, rolling your eyes, making faces, sticking out your tongue, writing notes, drawing pictures, flicking people off, using the third finger or a number of other hand signs that imply "loser," "crazy," or irreverent and sexual innuendos.

Psychological emotional bullying comes in the form of indirect abuse such as exclusion, isolation, rejection, turning your back on someone who is trying to talk with you, shunning, ostracizing, and ignoring. It may be subtle, or it may be overt. Sometimes these natural schisms form between girls who are becoming more interested in boys and girls who still want to spend most of their time with other girls. Frequently, however, this heartbreaking form of abuse is intentional and without apparent reason. While not exclusive to girls, this type of bullying is inflicted more habitually by female students.

We often tell children that when someone commits a crime in our society, we send them to prison. Prison officials had to come up with something worse than incarceration for those who break a law while they are jailed, so they created solitary confinement. One of the cruelest forms of punishment that humans can inflict on one another is total isolation. It appears that the two places in our society where isolation is most likely happen are prisons and playgrounds!

Some examples from students of nonverbal emotional bullying are: "Whenever this boy would see me at school, he would make a fist with one hand and then pound it into his other hand. He never hit me, but I never knew if he would try."

"One day when I was changing clothes in the locker room for gym, I opened my locker and there was a drawing of me taped inside the door. I will never forget it. It showed me naked—with a big head, big arms, big body, big legs and a very tiny you know what." All my friends were standing around waiting for me to open my locker. When I did, they howled with laughter. These were supposed to be my friends. You don't expect your friends to turn on you like that."

Here are some samples of psychological emotional bullying: "No one ever invited me to their birthday parties, so when my birthday came along, I sent an invitation to everyone in the class. My mom and I baked cupcakes for everyone and we put their names on with icing. We got gift bags for everyone and we planned some special games. It was going to be the best birthday I ever had. On the day of my party, I waited and waited and waited and no one came."

"I dreaded phys-ed! Whenever it came time to pick teams, I knew that I would be the last one picked because I wasn't good at athletics and nobody wanted to get stuck with me. Then when I would mess up and cause my team to lose the game, everyone would make the Loser sign with their fingers. I tried to get out of gym class whenever I could."

The concept of emotional bullying is the most challenging of the five types to transmit because it is the most elusive form of cruelty. As one child advocate, Dorothy Dean, stated, "Emotional abuse is the most difficult type of abuse to define and diagnose. Physical abuse, verbal abuse and some sexual abuse can be documented and verified. The victim, if old enough, can describe what occurred. Emotional abuse, however, is intangible. The wounds are internal but they may be more devastating and crippling than any other form of abuse."

Sexual Bullying

Sexual bullying has always included inappropriate touching and sexual harassment. Today's definition of sexual bullying, however, has to include the use of sexual language directed at students regarding homosexuality, which has caused tragic results.

Examples of physical sexual bullying that students have described include touching someone in an inappropriate place, lifting up a girl's skirt or pulling down a boy's pants, pushing a boy and a girl together so their bodies touch, brushing against a person on purpose, grabbing a girl's breasts, pinching someone's butt, pulling a girl's bra strap, kicking a boy in his private parts, or hugging or kissing someone when they don't wish to be hugged or kissed.

Students frequently use the term *harassment,* without knowing what the term means, but one student gave a very professional answer: "Sexual harassment is unwelcome sexual behavior that makes you feel uncomfortable or unsafe." One boy wanted to distinguish touching *with* consent from touching *without* consent. Our concern would be interpretation of consent, for example—"She said 'no' but she didn't really mean it," and then there is reluctant consent in order to be accepted or gain popularity.

One example that came to our attention was the case of a boy who was stripped down to his underwear in the locker room and then thrown out into the hall as students were going from one class to the next. This was described during a discussion with a large group of middle school students. When it was mentioned, all the students hooted with laughter except for one boy whose face was contorted in pain. It was obvious who had been "pantsed."

When elementary school students offered "rape" as an answer, Fried would remind them that she had asked for examples of sexual bullying at their age level and therefore rape was not appropriate for our discussion. However, on one such occasion, a teacher followed her out into the hall when the session was over and told her that one of the girls in the fifth grade had been raped. Fried no longer discounts "rape" as inappropriate.

Students have spoken of sexual bullying that is also emotional. This can come in the form of pressuring someone to engage in sexual activity that makes him or her feel uncomfortable. It can be certain hand and finger gestures, or licking lips in a suggestive way. One young girl reported that someone kept thrusting pictures of naked people in her face. It can be whistles or rude noises. Girls have also spoken about being manipulated or used so the male can brag about his sexual conquests to peers. Boys can be pressured by their peers to earn "stud" status. They feel they have to insist on having sex with a girl or pretend that they have, to escape being branded as gay.

One boy arranged to have a friend of his hide in his bedroom closet with a video camera where a hole had been drilled. The result was a videotape of himself and his girlfriend having sex, unbeknownst to her, to show to his friends.

Sexual emotional bullying can also be a form of gender discrimination—not allowing someone to do something because they are male or female, such as team sports. Students mention this with great frequency.

Some girls become very competitive about boys in middle school and high school. A lot of bullying between girls at that age revolves around boys. This territorial aspect of bullying appears to be more common among teenage girls than boys.

Most sexual bullying is male to female or male to male but it can also be female to female. A principal told us of a situation where she called thirty-five girls into her office to resolve a sexual bullying problem. The girls were ridiculing a girl whose breasts jiggled when she ran. The principal dealt with the incident by confronting the entire gym class and letting them know that such taunting would not be tolerated.

Many people who work with teenagers are concerned about the widespread practice of oral sex among teenagers. Even students as young as twelve and thirteen are experimenting with this activity. Many teenagers engaging in oral sex do not really consider this sex at all, or consider it a form of safe sex.

We think this warrants inclusion in our discussion of sexual bullying. Some might question whether oral sex is sexual bullying if it is voluntary and not coercive, but if young girls are unaware of the possible consequences of herpes, sexually transmitted diseases, and AIDS, or if they are willing to forfeit their health for the sake of popularity, we see this as sexual exploitation.

Then there is the category of sexual bullying that is verbal. In third or fourth grade, if boys and girls even have a conversation with someone of the opposite sex, kids will sing songs like: "Keith and Kayla sitting in a tree, k-i-s-s-i-n-g." By sixth grade it's dirty jokes and obscene phone calls. One boy spoke about some awful graffiti in the boys' bathroom. Guys would write on the walls that some girl was a "slut," and then other boys would add really nasty comments about things she supposedly did. He said, "These girls would die if they knew what was being written about them."

Sexual bullying can be calling someone the name of a body part or ridiculing someone because they have developed more quickly or more slowly than his or her peers. Girls have mentioned this on many occasions. They have spoken of being called "cows" or "pancakes." As young people approach puberty and hormonal changes take over, they become extremely sensitive about their bodies. It is a time of confusion, stress, and anxiety. Sexual bullying can be spreading sexual rumors about someone that are untrue but wholly believed because of the salacious interest.

Another facet of verbal sexual bullying is the use of words like *gay, queer, faggot, homo, lesbo, tramp, slut, whore, ho,* and worse. This kind of language is rampant and pervasive, beginning in elementary schools.

We used to be tentative about mentioning some of these words if they were not forthcoming from the students, but circumstances have changed our reluctance. In many cases of multiple school shootings, the particular form of taunting that pushed boys over the edge was the relentless tagging of being "gay," "homo," a "fag," a "pussy," or some other sexually pejorative term. Sometimes students will try to deny the meanness of the word *gay* by claiming that they were referring to the person as "happy." Our response to that disclaimer is to suggest that if you wish to offer a compliment for their cheerfulness, be sure to use words that can't be interpreted any other way. Dodging the slur is *not* acceptable.

In a discussion with seventh graders one morning, one boy asked if it was bullying to call someone gay who is gay. This led to a conversation about the climate in the school. Are students who are gay accepted by their peers? Do gay students feel comfortable acknowledging their sexual preference? Would a gay student hear the comment as intended humiliation? Our ongoing pitch to children is to emphasize the possible consequences of intentional hurtfulness. They need to know that if they inflict pain on someone, it can turn to rage, or it can turn to depression. Our task is to help them understand how important it is to stop the pain!

At a workshop conducted for professionals, a therapist who works with sex offenders reported to us that 75 percent of the sex offenders that she had worked with disclosed that they had been bullied about their sexuality when they were in school and felt they had to prove their sexuality to themselves and others.

These are challenging issues to address with students, and we know of teachers and administrators who would prefer to avoid them altogether. The fact that students consistently raise these issues with us, often taking great risks in front of their peers to do so, compels us to match their courage with our own. Too many innocent children pay a price for our unwillingness to confront the sexual behavior that happens in our schools.

"Sexting" or "sex-texting" is the most current teen aberration. We first heard about it from a teacher in a small Midwestern community before it appeared on national news, a few weeks later. It combines sexual and cyber bullying. Teen-age girls are using cell phones to capture nude or semi-nude photos of themselves and sending them to their boyfriends.

Jessica Logan sent such a picture to her boyfriend. When they broke up, he sent Jessica's picture to a group of girls. They disseminated the pictures, even to other school sites, and began posting nasty comments about Jessica, calling her a slut and a whore. Their relentless derision ultimately led to Jessica's suicide.

More recently, a young girl who sent a nude photo to a boyfriend, discovered that he sent it to all the members of the football team, who in turn dispersed it to countless others, and it ended up on the cell phone of the vice-principal of her school.

The widespread distribution of such nude photos has prompted prosecutors in some states, who are determined to put a stop to this practice, to charge these youngsters with child pornography. An under-age young girl who took a nude photo of herself has been charged with creating child pornography and the boyfriend who passed it on has been charged with distributing child pornography. A boy who took photos of his private parts and sent them to girls in his class is facing felony obscenity charges.

Being charged as a sex offender has life-long consequences. If any youths are convicted of this felony they will have to re-register as a sex offender wherever they move, and their contact with children will be monitored and limited. The repercussions are profoundly serious.

Some adults believe these matters should be handled by the school, the parents involved, and their children, before they are referred to the court system. Prosecutors are defending their harsh measures in hopes of setting an example with these kinds of cases in the early stages. They want to send the strongest message possible before this behavior gets out of hand.

Cyber Bullying

As complex and lethal as the more familiar forms of bullying are, the twenty-first century has brought with it an even more devastating, far reaching form of bullying, namely, cyber bullying. The anonymity and unlimited dissemination of this form of harassment takes cruelty to a level never imagined. Bullying at school now extends to bullying in your home, and consequently, there is no relief or sanctuary. Cyber bullying is a special challenge for schools because most of the bullying occurs on home computers, while the devastating effects impact the school environment.

According to Kowalski, Limber & Agatston, 2008, cyber bullying is defined as bullying through email, instant messaging, in a chat room, on a Web site, or through digital messages or images sent to a cell phone. Their important study indicates that the biggest jump in online activity occurs between sixth and seventh grade and that young girls are more likely to be online than boys and are more likely to use instant messaging.

Patchin and Hinduja define cyber bullying "as willful and repeated harm inflicted through the medium of electronic text. Computers with Internet access and cellular phones are the primary ways through which bullying occurs." In their research they found that about half of the victims reported being bullied in some way while in a chat room. In addition to chat rooms and Web sites, cyber bullies use text messages; steal passwords; engage in online stalking; post hurtful comments on MySpace, Zanga, and Facebook; post videos on YouTube; and manipulate any possible opportunity to use their tech savvy to be cruel.

WiredKids contends that cyber bullying has to have a minor on both sides, or at least have been instigated by a minor against another minor. Once adults become involved, it is plain and simple cyber harassment or cyber stalking. Adult cyber harassment or cyber stalking is never called cyber bullying. More information on this very important issue is included in Chapters Ten and Eleven.

We submit that posing these five types of bullying to students is essential if we want them to grasp the breadth and depth of peer abuse. The information they will divulge and the stories they will share will lay the groundwork for behavior changes that must occur.

Bringing children and adults to a more sophisticated understanding of the definitions and dimensions of bullying is imperative in any long-range plan to reduce and/or eliminate peer abuse.

Chapter 5

Perspectives on the Bullying Continuum

I couldn't believe how children were treating each other in the Center.

—Francis, Director of a Child Care Center

In a stunning statement Dorothy L. Espelage, Ph.D., reports that "in the fifteen years that I have studied bullying and other forms of youth aggression, the children have gotten younger and younger in their manifestations of these behaviors. The behaviors we saw in fifth-graders, we are now seeing in preschool playgroups. I think this is due in part to the introduction of technology to youth and their level of sophistication associated with their targeting each other." This is certainly an urgent wake up call to address the serious problem of bullying starting with early childhood education. Clearly, bullying behavior starts as early as preschool and must be addressed as soon as it is identified. Many factors influencing bullying among school age children play into early childhood bullying as well.

EARLY CHILDHOOD BULLYING

We are defining early childhood as birth through five years of age, the most impressionable years. "The formative early years are critical years, when traits of character are influenced and when young children gather and develop a strong sense of themselves and others." So states, Carol B. Hillman, author of "Before the School Bell Rings." She continues to write about the special qualities of this age—curiosity, exploration and many lessons learned from play. "Play is the way that children learn to be in charge, to be responsible. Through play, young children gain a sense of power."

Educators in childcare programs and preschools report that they have some students who are aggressive and domineering at this early stage and ask how to distinguish a bossy child from a bully. Bossiness crosses the line when it is affecting other children. It is also an excellent opportunity to teach young children how to stand up for themselves in an assertive way.

Another approach might be to assign a bossy child to be in charge of a project such as picking up all of the toys. S/he is told to give directions to each of the other children. When the project is completed, give praise for a leadership job well done. At the same time, praise all of the children who were good followers and speak about how important it is to be both a good leader and a good follower. The bossy child should continually be given the opportunity to demonstrate that s/he is learning to be a good leader *and* a good follower.

The bottom line is that the bossy child, if not nipped in the bud, may quickly become a bully. Young children must be taught that calling classmates names, taking toys, making threats, and being too bossy are all aspects of bullying.

Young children who become bullies often come from homes where they observe abuse, are victims of abuse, have little parental supervision, lack social skills, and experience harsh physical punishment. They often manifest antisocial behavior, signs of childhood depression, or may be very angry.

A teacher related a story that happened in her preschool. A petite bully, named Maxine, had already learned how to terrorize her peers. One morning, Maxine planted herself in front of Robbie, put her hands on her hips and emphatically told him that his mother was never going to come back for him. No words could cause more panic for a three year old. Robbie burst into tears. As the teacher ran over to console him, Juliet, a fellow three-year-old playmate, patted Robbie on his arm and assured him that his mommy would come and get him, just like she did every day. Robbie's tears and his bully disappeared. At a very young age, Juliet had already become a responsible witness.

Now the teacher focused on Maxine. She was given a strong empathy lesson and experienced an appropriate consequence. Bullying has a profound effect at all stages in life but particularly in the early years. Prevention and early intervention cannot be stressed enough.

BULLY FREE CLASSROOMS

Early childhood educators who have very little bullying in their classrooms attribute it to the fact that they teach social skills; they teach and model kindness, and they create an environment in which the young children feel safe.

It is a generally accepted fact that preschool children enter school with few if any social skills. They have to be taught the most basic social behavior of simply saying "Please" and "Thank you" at the appropriate time.

These educators meet their students at the classroom door and greet them by saying, "Good morning, Melinda," and wait for the young child to respond with "Good morning, Ms. Sunshine." The early childhood educator should encourage this very basic verbal social exchange with every student-to-student interaction and with every student-to-teacher interaction. Snack time and recess are also opportunities for teaching and practicing social skills that were taken for granted years ago. Snack time, "Please pass the cookies," and recess, "You can't say that you can't play," should teach these skills until they become second nature for these young students. When students learn to respect themselves and one another at a very early age, there is no need to bully.

Social skills are also learned through well supervised "play dates." In addition, play dates help preschool children develop friendships, which in turn help build confidence.

Good social skills, friends, and confidence are all factors that deter bullies.

POSITIVE SCHOOL ENVIRONMENT

Preschool and childcare buildings should be light, bright, and have a happy feel throughout. Children's artwork should be on the walls of the hallways as well as in the classrooms. The halls and classrooms could display posters, proverbs, or pictures of heroes. One poster we suggest would say: "Sticks and Stones Can Break Your Bones but Words Can Break Your Heart." Story time, arts and crafts, and games can be coordinated with the visuals.

Montessori educators worldwide find the peace table a very effective tool to prevent and combat bullying. On the Web site of The Montessori School of Tokyo we read "Children normally find it difficult to tell us and each other how they feel. The peace table plays an important part in our classroom; two children having a disagreement will normally decide to retreat to the peace table to discuss and solve their problem. Teaching peace involves finding a way to appreciate our differences and work together more effectively than ever."

Children do well in a structured environment, one in which they know what to expect and what is expected of them. Visitors are often surprised to see the ease with which these youngsters move from one activity to the next. Some children find these transitions more difficult than others, but that is part of the teaching/learning process of early childhood education.

Parents and educators must be mindful of the fact that young children can vary as much as two years in reaching milestones. Some acquire verbal skills earlier and lag behind in motor skills and vice versa. It is important to work through their strengths to help them acquire the skills that are more challenging for them. The more confident they feel about their abilities, the less likely they will be bullied. Early intervention is crucial for their mental health and for the safety of their classmates.

MIDDLE CHILDHOOD

The developmental stages of bullying behavior progress on a continuum. Many of the behaviors exhibited by preschool children continue into kindergarten and the early elementary grades. Middle childhood is the period between the ages of 6 and 12. In their book, *Development Contexts in Middle Childhood*, editors Aletha Huston and Marika Ripke "conclude that, although lasting individual differences are evident by the end of the preschool years, a child's developmental path in middle childhood contributes significantly to the adolescent and adult that he or she becomes. Families, peers, and the broader social and economic environment all make a difference for young people's future education, work and relationships with others."

"Kids in middle childhood think more abstractly, understand, for example that a person can be both nice and not nice . . . there is a kind of cognitive blooming . . . This is the time you develop industry, a sense of being able to do things, and explore things, or you develop the downside and the downside is inferiority. If you don't begin to expand your horizons and learn a lot of things, and learn the basics that school has to teach you, then you are vulnerable to long term inferiority, because you are going to feel that you can't do things."

Huston continues by pointing out "that it's not simply book learning. It's mastering the stuff we take for granted, like riding a bike, learning to swim and making friends. In fact, making friends may be one of the most important jobs of middle childhood. This is a time children really build a foundation of being able to relate to peers. Making friends, getting along with people your own age, that's critically important to your life."

Professor Huston is considered one of the leaders in the field of middle childhood. Much of her research is built on the landmark Columbia County Longitudinal Study discussed earlier. This study originated in 1960 by Leonard Eron, Ph.D. All third graders in the county—436 boys and 420 girls—as well as most of their parents were interviewed. Later, the students were asked, who the bullies and who the popular kids were.

There were actually ten questions on aggression, such as "Who pushes and shoves other children?" "Who says mean things?" "Who makes up stories and lies to get other children into trouble?" Students identified their classmates who exhibited these behaviors by circling their names.

The questions to identify the popular classmates included "Who would you like to have as your best friend?" "Who would you like to sit next to in class?"

As discussed earlier, the results of this longitudinal study found that by the time the original group was 48 years of age the early findings still held. Researchers were able to interview 523 of the original participants. They asked about occupation, education, income, marital status, mental health, their own children, and the behavior of their spouse. This information was gathered during a four-hour assessment that included an achievement test.

The Eron study has been significant for many years because of its important findings as well as for the amount of subsequent research that has been conducted in the area of middle childhood. In addition to Professor Huston's findings, we have the work of Dr. Eric F. Dubow, professor of psychology at Bowling Green State University and an adjunct researcher at the University of Michigan. Professor Dubow and a team of researchers at the University of Michigan conducted an extensive analysis of the Eron study. "It's obviously not true for every child, but a child's behavior at age 8 is relatively predictive of behavior in adolescence, and that in turn predicts educational status . . . It is the impact of aggressive behavior on educational status that appears to lead to low occupational success." Thus, the continuum from early childhood to middle childhood continues into adolescence and adulthood.

"This study and others like it come out of a growing awareness among psychologists, educators and policy makers that this period known as middle childhood between the ages of 6 and 12, has a far greater impact on making us who we are than earlier theorists acknowledged," wrote Jenni Laidman, Blade Science Writer, in her November 2006 article "Is age 8 too late?—Kids who don't play well with others may not be successful grown ups."

The results of this ongoing research affirm the importance of understanding and developing effective techniques for prevention and early intervention. There is increasing literature about the fact that bullies can also be targets and that popular students can become targets as well.

Megan, who is now in her fifties, recalled very clearly for us the influence that going from being popular to being bullied had on her life. She was very popular in eighth grade and then in ninth grade she became the target of a bully "who was much bigger than I was and who fought me to the ground. To this day I have no idea of why she chose me to be her target." Megan went on to graduate from a prestigious university, pursued a number of careers, and had several meaningful relationships but never married. Her adult life included numerous periods of severe depression, which she connected to her change in status, confusion, and fear in the ninth grade.

INTERNET BULLYING STARTS EARLY

A new phrase has entered our vocabulary: "Barbie Brats." The name applies to an overlooked group of kids—young children, only 6 or 8 or 10 years old, who bully other kids in real life or on the Internet," reports Louise Mysilk, LCSW. She also indicates that bullying among younger elementary school age children is on the rise. Studies show that three-quarters of children aged 8 to 11 say they have been bullied on the Internet.

The fact that Internet bullying starts at such a young age, must be a real wake-up call for parents, educators, school administrators, and mental health professionals. Middle childhood classrooms should have class rules agreed upon by the students at the beginning of the school year. A teacher-led discussion gives the students an opportunity to contribute to the rules and consequences and take ownership of them. Three to five rules seem to work best and should include the concepts of respect and responsibility. This process and enforcement are very effective for the creation of bully free elementary school classrooms.

Montessori schools find the peace table very effective for middle childhood students as well as for the preschool students. The students report that just the opportunity "to talk things through" is very helpful.

MIDDLE SCHOOL BULLYING

Bullying peaks in middle school, when students are 12 to 14 years old. Some middle schools begin with the sixth grade, some with seventh. Regardless, it can be a treacherous time of life. As one student said, "Middle school is senselessly evil."

The physical, emotional, and sexual development varies greatly. One student can be four feet and another two feet taller. With their hormones leaping all over the place, they are on an emotional roller coaster. They are moving toward independence but are still in limbo.

The American Academy of Child & Adolescent Psychiatry says that this stage is a time of experimentation, testing limits, and struggle for a sense of identity. Their intellectual interests expand, but they have limited thoughts of the future. They are awkward about their changing bodies and have an increased interest in sex.

All of this angst leads to thrashing around and lashing out at their peers. The taunting can be outrageous and relentless. Sexual bullying, especially around sexual language, is rampant and causes enormous pain.

The adults in authority at middle schools must keep a vigilant eye on the way students tyrannize each other. There is nothing more devastating for an adolescent male than to have his masculinity publicly challenged.

At the beginning of the school year, we advise that bullying in all of its forms be addressed, especially cyber bullying, and make it clear that it will not be tolerated. Spell out the consequences and how they will be enforced. Don't forget this is a time for testing limits—the sooner you make a rule, the sooner it will be challenged. Every adult must intervene at the first infraction and maintain authority throughout the year.

At the same time, keep in mind that these young people are searching for adults with whom they can confide. They have just left being in the embrace of one teacher a year for six years and now they are just one part of a mass. In conversations with teachers at this level, they work very hard to find a balance between being a sounding board and being firmly in control of the classroom. One teacher advises: "Don't show it when you're shocked and don't get into a power struggle. Don't ever call them "children"—that word grates. They love humor and appreciate honesty."

Above all, keep them safe. Middle school can be a very dangerous place and they desperately need your protection.

HIGH SCHOOL BULLYING

"According to recent studies, between 20–40 percent of U.S. teen-agers report being bullied three or more times during the last year. Between 7–15 percent report bullying others three or more times during the past year," writes Debbie Wilborn. She indicates that compared to nonbullying teens, bullies tend to:

- Have difficulty accepting criticism
- Have the need to be the center of attention
- Be more likely to drink alcohol and use drugs excessively
- Be at greater risk of being victimized themselves (about 50% of bullies are also victims at some point)
- Be at higher risk for mental health problems such as conduct disorder and attention deficit-hyperactivity disorder
- Be more likely to be antisocial in adulthood
- Be more likely to use violence in relationships
- Be more likely to get into trouble with the law.

Wilborn continues and points out that, compared to nonbullied teens, targets tend to:

- Be at higher risk for mental and physical health problems such as depression, stomachaches, and headaches
- Be absent from school more frequently because of bullying
- Continue to experience higher levels of anxiety through adulthood
- Have low self-worth
- Feel that control of their lives rests with someone else.

Research indicates that a majority of adolescents do not feel safe in school. These students maintain that teachers and other school personnel have "no clue" as to how much bullying behavior goes on every day in the hallways and other nonacademic venues, such as locker rooms, school grounds, and buses.

Although bullying may decrease during the senior high school years it is certainly more violent. With the statistics related above it is no wonder that students don't feel safe in school.

Warning signs for adolescents include the following:

- Shows a significant personality change and/or change in behavior
- Has a significant change in sleeping and/or eating habits
- Expresses fear about going to school
- Refuses to go to school
- Talks about suicide
- Attempts suicide or other forms of physical harm to self

Based on extensive research, James Garbarino and Ellen deLara wrote the following in their book on adolescents, "And Words Can Hurt Forever":

In summary, here are some of the signs to look for that indicate that your school system is not functioning as well as it needs to for kids to feel safe:

- When you hear kids saying, "There's nothing anybody can do to change it" (whether "it" is bullying, disrespectful interactions, or the school climate). These students are saying that they feel helpless. This encourages them to manufacture their own immature ways of feeling empowered, such as by bringing weapons for defense to school.
- When you hear kids say, "The teachers have no control, I put my trust in the other students." They are saying they cannot count on the adults to protect them. The feeling that they have to take matters into their own

hands encourages students to form groups for self-protection. Some will join healthier groups than others, who may end up in "gangs."

- When kids start saying, "Sometimes the teachers just walk by if there's a fight. And you know they hear all the terrible crap kids say to one another. They don't do anything about it." Kids are telling us that we are letting them down. They know adults are allowing and permitting a disrespectful, emotionally hostile environment.
- When the students (and some of the adults) start to say, "It's the druggies (or the Goths, or any other particular group) who are the problem in our school. If it weren't for them, everything would be okay here." When that happens, the members of the named group have become scapegoats; no one else needs to take responsibility for the disrespectful atmosphere of the school. This encourages continued taunting and bullying of the scapegoated group.
- When all is said and done, we must give up the comforting myth that except for a handful of "school shooters," our schools are safe. Schools abound with issues of psychological dangers and physical vulnerability.

ADOLESCENT DATING ABUSE

Adolescent dating abuse is certainly a serious manifestation of teen peer abuse. It has become a matter of such serious concern that "loveisrespectorg" (the National Teen Dating Abuse Helpline reports the following "dating abuse fast facts" based on findings of the March 2006 study commissioned by Liz Claiborne, Inc:

- 1 in 5 teens who have been in a serious relationship report being hit, slapped or pushed by a partner.
- 1 in 3 girls who have been in a serious relationship say they've been concerned about being physically hurt by their partner.
- 1 in 4 teens who have been in a serious relationship say their boyfriend or girlfriend has tried to prevent them from spending time with friends or family; the same number have been pressured to only spend time with their partner.
- 1 in 3 girls between the ages of 16 and 18 say sex is expected for people of their age if they're in a relationship; half of the teen girls who have experiences sexual pressure report they are afraid the relationship would break up if they did not give in.
- Nearly 1 in 4 girls in a relationship (23%) reported going further sexually than they wanted as a result of pressure.

These facts demand our immediate attention. Parents, teachers, and health professionals are once again urged to be aware of and immediately heed the following warning signs:

- Changes in teen's mood and/or personality
- Mental health issues such as depression and/or anxiety
- Withdrawal from family and friends in response to boyfriend's/girlfriend's demand to control their time
- Adolescent is no longer interested in hobbies or other activities that were previously of great interest.
- Expressions of jealousy
- Strong students whose grades are obviously falling
- Unexplained injuries should never be ignored
- Name-calling and put-downs in public and private
- Display of anger and violent behavior such as punching, grabbing, pushing, slapping, hitting, shoving
- Same type of name calling we see in all types of peer abuse: put downs, making the partner feel bad about herself/himself, telling their partner that no one else would date her/him or that they are ugly or fat or stupid, and on and on.

Parents or a significant adult in the adolescent's life must teach the teen to ask herself/himself the following questions:

- Do you strike out at your girlfriend/boyfriend?
- Does s/he make you feel uncomfortable in any way?
- Does s/he demand that you change your behavior to keep her/him happy?
- Do you have a problem controlling your anger?
- Have you hit or hurt someone you care about?

It is imperative that adolescents in abusive relationships get protection and help immediately. It is also imperative to engage students to take action in their own behalf.

An amazing conference about bullying, "When Push Comes to Shove—Finding Solutions to Bullying Behavior," took place in Topeka, Kansas, in early 2009, and Fried was a keynote speaker. The goal was to empower high school students to become advocates for change in their own schools. January Scott, conference coordinator, recruited students from all over the community to attend, and 30 student leaders from three high schools and one middle school were trained prior to the conference to be small group facilitators.

One hundred twenty adults, including principals, counselors, teachers, and parents, and 118 students came together to integrate information they had learned from keynote speakers and make commitments to make a difference upon their return to their schools. The evaluations indicated that the students left the conference with changed perspectives about the seriousness of bullying. They felt a greater compassion for students who were bullied, a deeper commitment to intervene when their friends were bullying, and were highly motivated to become more involved in bullying prevention.

CREATING STRONG AMERICAN SCHOOLS

Creating strong American schools is a key factor in banishing bullying behavior from our classrooms at all academic levels, early childhood education, middle childhood, and adolescent secondary schools. Students must be intellectually engaged at their appropriate instructional level by effective teachers, equipped to teach them the knowledge and skills in preparation for college, jobs, and life. Our schools must be able to provide an environment that promises success for the gifted and talented, for the average student, as well as the struggling student who needs one-on-one attention.

While the United States once had the best graduation rate in the world, today it ranks only twentieth among top developed countries as reported by the Organization for Economic Cooperation in 2008. Seventy percent of eighth graders are not proficient in reading—and most will never catch up. In the June 5, 2008, issue of *Education Week* we read that, "This spring, 1.2 million students will fail to graduate with their peers." This type of failure is a breeding ground for bullies and bullying behavior. There are a number of very successful programs around the country that are building strong American schools. The organization, Strong American Schools, a project of Rockefeller Philanthropy Advisors, is a nonpartisan campaign supported by the Eli and Edythe Broad Foundation and the Bill & Melinda Gates Foundation promoting sound education policies for all Americans. It is a public awareness and action campaign in support of education reform. Strong American Schools has published a Toolkit almost 100 pages long to enable parents, educators, and concerned citizens as well as elected government officials to bring about education reform from the grassroots up.

The Toolkit lays out a threefold approach to strengthen our schools:

1. American education standards. Regardless of where they live, every student needs a strong curriculum in subjects such as math and English.
2. Effective teachers in every classroom. We need to enable teachers to improve their skills, measure teachers' performance in the classroom, and

pay them more if they produce superior results or take on challenging assignments.
3. More time and support for learning. We need to provide successful and struggling students alike more time for in-depth learning and greater personal attention.

"Rigorous standards, effective teaching, and time and support for learning are among the most important resources that any school can provide its students. They are the backbone of a strong education system. And they matter at all levels—from kindergarten through high school—for students from all walks of life."

An outstanding example of highly successful schools is the KIPP Schools founded in 1994 in the Bronx by David Levin and Michael Feinberg. Now 66 strong, these Knowledge is Power Program schools start the day at 7:30 a.m. and run until 5:00 p.m. Classes are held every other Saturday and students attend summer sessions for three weeks. KIPP students get 60 percent more class time than their peers. The results are astounding: In Washington, D.C., KIPP fifth graders improved so much in just one year that they rose from the bottom 15 percent to the top 25 percent of students in the nation.

Teachers have a bigger impact on students' learning than anything else. They are the single, greatest "natural resource" in education, and yet they are underpaid, underappreciated, and in many cases underprepared to meet the challenges in today's schools. It is a well-known fact that we are simply not attracting our best and brightest students to go into the field of education. One cannot expect a C college education major to become an A teacher.

The Teacher Advancement Program (TAP) has been in operation since 2000. It was designed to attract, develop, motivate, and retain talented teachers. Now a part of the National Institute of Excellence in Teaching (NIET) TAP operates in more than 130 schools in 14 states and Washington, D.C. TAP involves 4,000 teachers and 60,000 students.

Another program designed to attract talented teachers is Teach for America, founded by Wendy Kopp when she graduated from Princeton. She believed that highly motivated college graduates, similar to people who joined the Peace Corps, could be recruited to commit to two years of teaching in urban and rural schools. Thousands of young people have proven her right.

Many of these young volunteers stay in the teaching field as a result of their experience, even though most of them do not have degrees in education. Those who pursue other careers insist that their powerful experience with Teach for America will be an indelible part of their lives, and they will carry the need for educational reform into their future, whatever they may do.

Chapter 6

Helping Students with Special Needs Achieve Success

Every day is a battle for me. I wish I didn't have all these problems. Why
can't they just leave me alone?

—Stewart, a special-needs student

Given all that special needs students have to deal with, they certainly don't
need to be forced to deal with bullies as well. Yet people who are different
often become the targets of bullies, and special needs students are frequently
perceived as different.

They might be gifted and talented, learning disabled, twice exceptional,
autistic, ADD, ADHD, or visually or hearing impaired. In many classrooms
there are students who are very protective of their special needs classmates,
but in some classrooms bullies try to take over.

Early diagnosis and intervention for a disease such as cancer can result in
a cure or long-term remission. Early diagnosis and intervention cannot cure
learning disabilities. There is no known cure for learning disabilities. However, the route to productivity for students with learning disabilities depends
on early detection and appropriate intervention.

Here are just a few examples of famous people who were able to com-
pensate for their disabilities: dyslexia—Presidents George Washington and
Woodrow Wilson, Tom Cruise, Patricia Palacco, and Vice President Nelson
Rockefeller, who is said to have memorized every speech because of his
concern about his inability to read the words; learning disability—Winston
Churchill, Walt Disney, Alexander Graham Bell, and Thomas Edison, who
didn't learn to read until he was 12 years old; Downs syndrome—Chris
Burke; hearing impaired—Marlee Matlin; manic-depressive—Patty Duke.

59

A graphic example of an individual who was able to compensate for his disability is Jim Abbott, who was born without one hand and yet was able to win Olympic gold in 1988 and became an outstanding major league pitcher. We could share literally hundreds of stories about famous people who learned to compensate for their disabilities and made outstanding contributions to humanity. We encourage you to go onto the Internet and input "famous people with disabilities" to read some of the fascinating stories about these famous individuals and in some cases how they suffered at the hands of bullies.

Bullies don't usually target confident classmates. Helping special needs students succeed and eliminating their "differentness" is vital to reducing the target population of bullies. That is why early diagnosis and intervention is so important to teach these students how to compensate for their disabilities.

As mentioned earlier we must acknowledge that there are children who are more likely to become bullies because of inborn traits, such as those who were crack babies, who suffered from fetal alcohol syndrome, and some children with attention deficit disorder (ADD) or attention deficit hyperactivity disorder (ADHD) whose disruptive behavior patterns may have a biological basis. They often become targets, as well.

Provocative targets create tension by irritating and annoying others and are more likely to fight back when attacked. Provocative targets may have ADHD, Asperger's syndrome, or learning disabilities that prevent them from picking up on social cues other children intuitively understand. These children can irritate others without even realizing it. Many parents have moved their children with special needs from one school to another, year after year, because of their ongoing pain. These children are extraordinarily bright and talented in many ways but suffer from inborn traits that they have not been able to control.

THE MEDICATION DEBATE

Ritalin makes it possible for some of these children to accommodate to the classroom environment, control their actions and interactions, and contain bullying behavior. Two widely used drugs, Concerta and Adderall XR, last twelve to fourteen hours and spare children the embarrassment of leaving the classroom to receive a dose of Ritalin, which lasts only four or five hours.

While the majority of families with children who are diagnosed with ADD or ADHD are grateful for the benefits of these drugs, it is important to recognize that there has been much concern expressed about medicating some children unnecessarily. Numerous articles have illustrated cases where parents preferred to "drugulate" their children's behavior rather than deal with the causes. We have interviewed several pediatricians who report seeing "miracles occur" with patients who are correctly diagnosed and appropriate medication prescribed.

Some parents of children with ADD or ADHD are finding a therapeutic element in karate and other forms of martial arts. Many doctors support this idea, as do several national nonprofit resource groups for people with the disorder, including the National Attention Deficit Disorder Association and Children and Adults with Attention-Deficit/Hyperactivity Disorder. They say that such courses help ease the symptoms of the disorder: impulsiveness, inability to concentrate, and, in some cases, hyperactivity. Other experts who say that it is nothing more than wishful thinking, however, dismiss this theory. They point to a lack of medical evidence to back up the theory.

MAJOR CONCERN ABOUT BULLYING OF SPECIAL NEEDS STUDENTS

The depth of concern about the abuse of special needs students is underscored by the wide range of participants in sessions on bullying that Sosland conducts at the annual state conference of the Missouri Learning Disabilities Association. Parents and educators from the field of early childhood education through high school come to these sessions eager for information to help their special needs students. Parents come expressing frustration with teachers and administrators who ignore their plea for help. Others share triumphs. Educators include classroom teachers, administrators, resource teachers, and mental health professionals, who express growing concern about the marked increase in bullying they observe, particularly cyber bullying. They are also looking for guidance on how to deal with parents of bullies. Strategies for children who have special needs to deal with bullies are listed in Chapter Eight, Change Agents, under the heading of Special Education Teachers.

CORRECT DIAGNOSIS

In many cases special needs students' needs are not identified and diagnosed. This often leads to unnecessary frustration and failure in the classroom. Unknowing parents will often say to them, "I know you can do it, if you would just try harder," but this just makes matters worse because it continues to make the students feel like failures. In the meantime, it makes them more apt to be targets of bullies.

The way to break this cycle is to prove to these students that they can be successful. We learned this important lesson from an eighth grade student, Candy, who was reading at the third grade level when we first met her in a middle school that was formerly a feeder school to a distinguished college-prep public high school. As the neighborhood changed, students entered the middle school from low income, non–college educated households.

The faculty refused to change the curriculum to meet the needs of the student body. As one teacher put it, "I have always taught *Animal Farm* in eighth grade and I will continue to do so," even though some of her students were reading at the third grade level. She was teaching, but her students were not learning and they were cutting class.

The school was located in a commercial area and some of the students were actually shoplifting. The shop owners got together, pooled some money, and came to the University Reading Education Department to ask for help. As a result, we developed a sixteen-week program where we met with small groups of students for one hour twice a week, teaching them the basic reading skills that they had missed.

THREE STEP PROCESS

In conjunction with this project, we designed a three-step process—observation, evaluation, and intervention. The first step was teacher observation. Teachers were asked to observe the students and refer those students who might best benefit from our program. Next we evaluated each student and established his or her respective instructional levels, and then we began our intervention.

The students gained an average of two years in their reading levels during the sixteen-week program, which is true of similar programs as well. We asked the student who started at the third grade level and scored at the eighth grade level by the end of the program how she managed such an increase. Her response was "You showed me that I could learn to read. I had given up on ever improving my reading skills but each week I got better in the work I did with you. I realized I could learn, and I did." We were so impressed with her achievement we followed up with her in high school and found that she was continuing to experience success at grade level.

ANNIE'S STORY

We received a call at the university from a fourth grade teacher inquiring whether we had an education major who might tutor one of her students who wasn't learning to read even though she was being taught at a second reading level. The teacher told us that she had requested a battery of tests for Annie because she was puzzled by her lack of progress learning to read. She questioned the results, which pegged Annie's IQ score as a slow learner, which is why she called us.

We checked Annie's record and found that she had had a battery of tests in first grade and at that time her IQ was average and she had been diagnosed with a learning disability. For some reason, Annie's learning disability had not been addressed, and academically, she fell further and further behind each year.

We asked Annie's teacher how she knew that Annie was not a slow learner and she replied," I have been teaching for fifteen years and I could tell by looking into her eyes. I have had enough students who are slow learners and they have a dull look which was not true of Annie." This is a graphic example of the efficacy of teacher observation. One of our students accepted the assignment to tutor Annie, but before she began, she gave Annie a reading evaluation, Step Two of our process. The evaluation indicated that Annie was reading at the pre-primer level and not at the second grade level.

Step Three, the intervention process, began when our student started to reteach Annie at the appropriate pre-primer level. Annie quickly advanced with each tutoring session. Our student's evaluation of Annie allowed her to address Annie's learning disability at the appropriate instructional level, an important key to success.

TOOLS FOR EVALUATION—THE INFORMAL READING INVENTORY

One of the best tools for evaluating reading levels is the Informal Reading Inventory, which can be administered in 12–15 minutes and allows the teacher, clinician, or parent who does the administration to observe the student in the process of reading. The Inventory establishes the student's Independent Reading Level, that level at which the student can read without assistance; the Instructional Level, that level at which the student should be taught; and the Frustration level, that level at which the student should NEVER be taught. The Listening Capacity is the final level, which measures the student's achievement potential, once the reading disability is addressed.

Reading is a skill that must be practiced just like any other skill, tennis, basketball, or piano. The Independent Reading Level is that level at which a student should practice reading and read for pleasure. The Instructional Level is the appropriate level to teach reading skills commensurate with the student's intellectual capacity. Annie, unfortunately, was being taught at her Frustration Level, which is why she was not able to learn. Finally, Annie's Listening Capacity was at the fifth grade reading level even though she was in the fourth grade. Looking back at her history we found that she had been retained one year and really should have been in the fifth grade. It is obvious that she had the capacity to do grade level work with the proper intervention. Annie almost fell through the cracks but a talented teacher rescued her. We urge parents to be strong advocates for their children if they feel that they might be falling through the cracks.

AN ASSESSMENT OF LETTER NAME KNOWLEDGE

Another very simple instrument for evaluation of students with learning disabilities is a test of letter names, upper case and lower case. The student is asked to read the letters that are not in alphabetical order. Directions for the administration are found in Appendix D. In a special project at the Juvenile Justice Center, Sosland gave a battery of reading instruments to 20 seventh grade boys. Five of the 20 could not read all the letters on the test of alphabet knowledge and of course their reading levels on the Informal Reading Inventory were very low. Sosland often described these results in her classes and one student who had a son in a suburban high school who continued to experience difficulty reading, administered this test to her son only to discover that he, indeed, could not read all the letters.

During the time that we were writing this book Sosland had a referral by a parent of a first grader who was experiencing difficulty learning to read. A test of letter names indicated that he had not mastered the letters of the alphabet, ending the alphabet song with the letter order "wyvxuz." He also confused b/d and p/q, common errors, but which need to be corrected before a student can learn to read competently. Parents and teachers should not assume that a first grader has mastered the alphabet and are urged to use the simple test of letter names to assess mastery of the alphabet.

Tom, Sosland's first student at the University Reading Clinic was a seventh grader reading at the fourth grade level. He was one of seven children, all high academic achievers, so his reading problems created emotional problems as well. In addition, his older brother, a source of pain, which he discussed in each tutoring session, taunted him mercilessly. Sosland discovered very quickly that he confused the letters g and j. Once she retaught these two letters, she was able to reteach other reading skills and the student began to enjoy reading. By practicing at his Independent Reading Level, he was able to read at grade level within a year. Tom progressed from the fourth grade level to the eighth grade level by the time he entered eighth grade. When this occurred, the sibling stopped the taunting.

WEPMAN TEST OF AUDITORY DISCRIMINATION

Another key component to ensure reading competence, which is the foundation on which academic success is built, is auditory discrimination. The Wepman Test of Auditory Discrimination is very easy to administer and students really enjoy doing this exercise.

Finally, we would recommend a Multiple Intelligences Inventory. Students enjoy taking this Inventory and it allows intervention to take place working through the student's strengths. There are more that 700 Multiple Intelligences Inventories available on the Internet. Readers are encouraged to select one that is appropriate for their student or child.

This battery of instruments can be administered in the classroom and provides a wealth of information for students, parents, and teachers. The information will enable a program of intervention to be available for the special needs student even if they don't qualify for special services.

INDIVIDUALIZED ATTENTION

Students, such as Candy, Annie, and the boys at the Juvenile Justice Center, who have fallen so far behind must have individualized instruction, be taught at their appropriate Instructional Level, and develop their academic skills through Independent practice.

Individualized instruction can take place with one-on-one tutoring. Student tutors from nearby colleges and universities, peer tutors, and adult volunteers are all valuable personal resources that have proven to be very successful. The tutoring sessions are very important, but equally important is the Independent practice that will only happen when students are motivated to succeed. We have come full circle to Candy's lesson about showing—not telling—students who are failing that they can learn.

Dr. Sidney Pakula, a revered pediatrician in Kansas City for many decades, told Sosland that he saw a thousand cases of reading problems in his practice each year. After he and a number of colleagues referred these patients for educational evaluation for many years, they decided to develop a screening instrument for pediatricians to administer in their own offices. This was during the period of "the great debate over phonics versus whole word instruction."

Dr. Pakula and his colleagues discovered that most of the students who were experiencing difficulty learning to read were in classrooms where instruction did not match their learning mode. Some students were being taught to read in a phonics program who would have done better with a whole word approach, and some students who were in classes using the whole word approach were much more successful when taught using a phonics approach. Today, we recommend using an eclectic approach that combines phonics and the whole word approach to reading instruction.

There is much to be learned from countries abroad. Linda Darling-Hammond, a professor of Education at Stanford University, has collected valuable research about the extent of resources that are being poured into teacher training and support in Asia, Australia, New Zealand, Canada, Finland, Sweden, Norway, and the Netherlands.

They are prepared more extensively and are well paid in relation to competing occupations. All teacher candidates in Finland, Sweden, Norway, and the Netherlands receive two to three years of graduate level preparation for teaching, at government expense, plus a living stipend.

Finland has been a poster child for school improvement. Teachers learn how to create programs that engage students in research and inquiry on a regular basis. There, training focuses on how to teach students who learn in different ways—including those with special needs.

PARENT ADVOCACY

Parents need to be aware of the type of instruction their children are receiving. In some cases the nature of the delivery instruction does not match the child's learning style, which causes an academic problem, which then creates a child with special needs, and can snowball into a bullying situation.

Over the years Sosland has had a number of referrals for educational evaluation by parents of kindergartners who reported that their young children who had been toilet trained for two to three years were suddenly bedwetting. In one case the parents realized that the bedwetting stopped when they were out of town for spring break and away from school. These were all very bright children who found themselves in kindergarten situations that were highly stressful, including bullying.

All the bullying literature, at all levels, stresses the importance of communication with your children. This is easier during the early years as opposed to adolescence, but if it can be maintained throughout the child rearing years, parents will be able to intervene on their children's behalf when necessary. Red flags, such as a return of bedwetting, loss of appetite, or stomach aches when it is time to leave for school, should be heeded immediately.

TWICE-EXCEPTIONAL STUDENTS

Although the term "at-risk students" has been used to describe a variety of the school population, it is most commonly used to identify low achievers who are "at-risk" of becoming dropouts, who may become adolescent suicides, participate in substance abuse, and become teenage parents. Then there are students who are "at-risk" precisely because they were overlooked as being "at-risk." These students are both learning disabled and gifted/academically talented. They are twice-exceptional.

The learning disability may mask the academic talent and the academic talent may mask the learning disability. These students often appear to be average or labeled as underachievers. There is no fault with being average, but when a student who is twice-exceptional is mislabeled as average, neither the special needs of the learning disability nor of the giftedness is met.

One of the most common deficits that may "mask" the ability of a bright student is that of fine motor control, which interferes with the ability to get ideas from the head to the paper. Some students have difficulty remembering how to form the letters while others have difficulty using the muscles necessary for handwriting. In any case, the word processor has been a helpful tool for some of these students; others have used the tape recorder to help them compensate for their disabilities.

These students often become behavior problems in the classroom. For example, Jon, a second grader in a private school was acting out and very disruptive in class. Teachers and administrators attributed his behavior to "being the youngest very spoiled child" in an upper income family. However his parents insisted that Jon have an educational evaluation and these test results indicated that Jon was reading at the eighth grade level but was being taught from a second grade basal reading program. He also had a subtle fine motor problem that kept him from completing writing assignments to his teacher's satisfaction.

Giving Jon eighth level reading material and adjusting for his fine motor skills deficit eliminated his negative behavior within a week. How long could any student, or adult for that matter, endure reading six levels below what he was capable of reading in class day after day without acting out in frustration? Clearly, the behavior was a cry for help, which Jon, fortunately, received. Acting out behavior in class and/or at home often is another red flag that should alert adults to a student's special needs problem. It is imperative to respond to the symptom by looking for the cause of the behavior.

Fine motor deficits caused academic problems for Edward, a bright high school student. He was being tutored in math because he continued to fail the math quizzes. Edward insisted that he understood the math concepts, though he was unable to pass the tests. When Edward's mother checked with the math teacher, the instructor confirmed her son's mastery of the math concepts in spite of his test scores.

The mother tried, to no avail, to persuade the teacher to take the student's fine motor issues into consideration. The teacher refused, on the grounds that "it wouldn't be fair to the other students." The mother countered "But the other students don't have a learning disability!" Over the years as we have advocated for individual special needs students from preschool through graduate school we have been told, "But it wouldn't be fair to the other students." In each case we have repeated, "But the other students don't have a learning disability" and tried to explain the need to help the students to compensate for that disability. Any educator from early childhood through graduate school who doesn't know or understand the difference between special needs students and regular students should not be in any classroom. This lack of professionalism underscores the importance of placing well-prepared educators in our schools, which is advocated by those who are calling for school reform. We owe this to our students and to ensure a well-educated population for the future of our country.

Edward's experience raised the important question of whether we are testing for understanding and knowledge or for the ability to write a quiz. If teachers understand the fact that among students there is a certain population who have deficits for which they must compensate we can avoid many problems for these students.

Some twice-exceptional students may be ADHD, discussed earlier in this chapter. Others may have language disorders, which interfere with their ability to follow oral instructions, follow auditory lessons presented orally, or express themselves orally. There are students who manifest just the opposite problem, that of spatial orientation who have difficulty processing information visually. These are often the students who make brilliant contributions to classroom discussions but experience reading difficulties. Some students may have difficulty retrieving information from memory.

Sequencing problems often lead bright students to experience difficulty as does lack of organizational skills. These same students have intellectual capacities that place them in the gifted and talented range. They often have very large vocabularies, may have been early readers, and have unusual language skills. Some of these students have long attentions spans, unusual persistence, and concentration. They learn quickly and retain vast amounts of information. These students require far less practice to master learning. They think deeply, are creative, have a broad range of varied interests, are curious, and willing to take risks and experiment.

This is just a very brief overview of the types of deficits bright students may experience that then makes them twice-exceptional. How do we meet the special learning needs of these unique students?

A SPECIAL TEACHER MEETS SPECIAL NEEDS

Pat Antonopoulos, a kindergarten teacher in a suburban school district, did an Independent Research project with Sosland to try to answer this question. She developed what she called "The Center Approach" to meet the diverse needs of 46 children ranging in chronological age from 5.1 years to 6.2 years and an I.Q. range of 82 to 164. The morning session of the kindergarten had 24 students and the afternoon session had 22 students. Each center had activities that encouraged creativity for all developmental levels. The activities also encouraged logical thinking, information processing, and detail recall. Many of the activities are verbal, easily accomplished with few materials, and exciting for the children.

Centers, also known as learning centers, give teachers the opportunity to teach to their students' strengths and give students the opportunity to make choices. Centers can be designed for individual work or group activities.

For the early childhood classroom we recommend a literacy center where children can curl up with a book or practice writing their letters, an art center, a drama center with dress up clothes, a science center, a sand and water table, and many preschools now have a computer in each classroom. Some children tend to favor one center. If that is the case, teacher guidance usually encourages the student to try other centers as well.

Similar centers are created by teachers in middle childhood classes on a more advanced level. Incorporation of learning centers varies from classroom to classroom depending on the teacher's approach to teaching.

These centers allow each student to function at his/her ability level. At the end of the school year each child thought that he/she was Mrs. Antonopoulos' favorite student and each child felt successful. This kindergarten teacher said she would never go back to her former way of teaching. Her work was cutting edge some twenty years ago and has proven to help all students at all grade levels, including special needs students, achieve success over these many years.

Chapter 6

GIFTED AND TALENTED STUDENTS

Unusually gifted and talented students also have special needs. We tend to equate special needs only with children who are physically, academically, or neurologically challenged, but gifted and talented children deserve extra attention, especially when it comes to bullying. More than two-thirds of academically talented eighth graders say they have been bullied at school, and nearly one-third harbored violent thoughts as a result, according to a study believed to be the first to examine the prevalence and impact of bullying in a group some experts regard as particularly vulnerable.

The study, published in the Gifted Child Quarterly, involved 432 students in 11 states who had been identified by their school systems as gifted. Jean Sunde Peterson, an associate professor at Purdue University, sought to explore whether harassing behavior affected gifted children differently.

"All children are affected adversely by bullying, but gifted children differ from other children in significant ways. Many are intense, sensitive and stressed by their own and others' high expectations and their ability, interests and behavior may make them more vulnerable. Additionally, social justice issues are very important to them and they struggle to make sense of cruelty and aggression."

One of the most alarming findings of the research involved the frequency of violent thoughts. By eighth grade approximately 37 percent of boys and 23 percent of girls in the study reported having unspecified violent thoughts in response to being bullied; 11 percent admitted that they resorted to violence.

Gifted students are frequently the object of derision and isolation by their peers because of jealousy and perceived differences. Reinforcing our concern about children who turn their pain inward, is the example of J. Daniel Scruggs, a slightly built Connecticut middle school student with an I.Q. of 139. When he could no longer cope with the relentless abuse he received from his classmates, including making him eat his lunch off of the cafeteria floor, he chose to commit suicide.

A conversation with an academically gifted student, Allise, added an additional perspective. Gifted students tend to bully themselves. They put enormous pressure on themselves to maintain their exceedingly high standards. This causes high levels of stress and anxiety, even physical extremes such as heart palpitations and fainting. These students are not homicidal or suicidal but require special support to conquer the issues they experience.

Allise was fortunate to have a school counselor, Mrs. Nikki Currie, who created "Tool Boxes" for a number of high achieving students. Each student had his/her own tool box that included unique contents to help them calm down. Allise was given breathing exercises that she could focus on when she began to feel nervous. Mrs. Currie told her to count her breaths and use accompanying hand signs that wouldn't be obvious to others. If that didn't work, she suggested that Allise scratch her ankles, because it's harder to faint when your head is below your heart. Additionally, Mrs. Currie signed a permanent pass for Allise that she could use to leave her classroom, when necessary, knowing that Allise would never abuse the privilege.

School assemblies could be very anxiety producing. If the commotion was causing a reaction, a hand signal from Allise activated the counselor to bring a pass to her teacher, requesting that Allise leave the auditorium. More than the amazing solutions that continued to surface for each new challenge was the constancy that the counselor represented. She never doubted that there wasn't a way to handle each predicament and her students knew that she would find it, somehow. The spirit of confidence she radiated to them was indispensable.

We hope this information will inspire parents, teachers, and university students to become strong advocates for these special students who often become targets of bullies. Working in synchrony, we can break the cycle of pain, rage, and revenge.

Chapter 7

The Challenge of Changing
the Culture

I think if everyone stopped bullying it would be a lot funner place to be.

—Jimmy, a student

Changing the culture. Three little words. One enormous challenge. Many years ago, a workshop leader at a public health conference described a public health approach to addressing community problems. The workshop presenter related the story of a village where many of the people had dysentery. Two approaches were being considered. The individual approach was to treat every person who had an intestinal disorder, the second was a community approach—to invest in a sewer system.

The bullying disorder that ravages many of our schools requires both approaches. We must find a way to identify and treat the infected children, both the targets and the bullies who are in pain. At the same time, we must create the equivalent of a sewer system to address the cause of the problem, which is to change the culture of the school community. This chapter focuses on the latter approach.

There is much that we can learn from Malcolm Gladwell's book, "*The Tipping Point*." In his book, Gladwell talks about the factors involved when a particular idea or trend becomes contagious, when it bursts out of its contained state and spreads like a virus. He refers to this mysterious transformation as an epidemic. He is fascinated by the one dramatic moment in an epidemic when everything can change all at once and becomes the tipping point.

Consider bullying as it relates to Gladwell's observation. How does a particular school atmosphere encourage mean-spirited behavior? At what point do a few students pick up on cues that encourage them to bully freely and become a determining factor in the level of accepted cruelty? Even more importantly, how can a school where bullying has become an epidemic rally to create an atmosphere where it is "cool to be kind" rather than "cool to be cruel?"

THREE AGENTS OF CHANGE

Gladwell claims that there are three agents of change—the Law of the Few, the Stickiness Factor, and the Power of Context. The Law of the Few demonstrates the power of a few people to set an epidemic into motion—a disease epidemic or a social epidemic, a negative epidemic or a positive one. An example of a negative disease epidemic would be the flu epidemic of 1918, which was first observed in the spring of that year. Had it been contained originally, when the first cases were diagnosed, the results might have been different, but by the end of the year its effects had caused the deaths of between 20 and 40 million people worldwide.

On the positive side, Gladwell points to a few people who have the capacity to set a social epidemic in motion. A most celebrated example of word-of-mouth contagion is Paul Revere. Astride his horse, he traveled thirteen miles in two hours and knocked on doors in every town along the way. His famous warning, "The British are coming," was heeded by local leaders who spread the word. By the time the British arrived, they were met with fierce resistance.

A most intriguing fact is that a man named William Dawes set out with the same message in a different direction but for the most part he was ignored. Why? Dawes didn't have the social standing and credibility that Revere did. This piece of information is very relevant when we relate Gladwell's account to our concerns about bullying and the power of a few respected students to change the bullies.

We offer another example of a positive social epidemic. It is the cultural revolution that occurred around smoking. There was a time when smoking was considered to be kind of sexy and romantic. The health issues were not yet exposed, and the tobacco industry had a grip on public consumption with its expertly crafted marketing techniques.

The amazing shift prompted by lawsuits, personal decisions, and policies banning smoking in public areas is absolutely phenomenal. Who would have imagined that smoking—an imbedded behavior pattern and even an addiction for some—could be prohibited in public spaces? The shift, championed by only a few in the beginning, brought about a dramatic change in our society.

The Stickiness Factor that Gladwell identifies looks at the elements that cause a message to stay with us rather than go in one ear and out the other. A most interesting example was an experiment conducted by the social psychologist Howard Levanthal in the 1960s. His goal was to persuade a group of college seniors at Yale University to get a free tetanus shot.

The students were divided into groups and given different booklets. One booklet was a "high-fear" version, indicating all the possible consequences if a tetanus shot was not received, including vivid photographs of catheters, tubes, and wounds. Another booklet, the "low fear" version had no photographs, and the verbal imagery was toned down considerably.

When Levanthal looked at the results of how many students had actually gone to the health center to obtain shots, a mere three percent had taken action. Neither approach had "stuck." When they redid the experiment and included a map of the campus with the health center circled and the times that the shots were available, twenty-eight percent of the students took advantage of the inoculation. There were an equal number of students from the "high-fear" and the "low-fear" groups. The stickiness factor occurred when the information that was given was both practical and personal. According to Gladwell, for the Stickiness factor to transfer to an epidemic, "ideas have to be memorable and move us to action." So it is with bullying. We must mobilize students with stories that touch them and solutions within their reach.

The last of Gladwell's agents of change is the Power of Context. A sterling example is the Broken Windows theory, referenced in *The Tipping Point*, which was the brainchild of James Q. Wilson and George Kelling, criminologists, in 1982. They maintain that when a sense of disorder in a community is prevalent—such as broken windows that aren't repaired, graffiti that isn't erased, litter that isn't picked up—vandals will feel freer to abuse the rights of others. The residents will perceive that no one cares and no one is in charge. Perception has a strong influence on behavior.

Wilson and Kelling recommend that little problems be repaired as soon as possible. Their premise is that an epidemic can be reversed when attention is paid to the smallest details.

An amazing example is the city of New York in the early 1990s. When Rudolph Giuliani became Mayor, he appointed William Bratton as Chief of the New York City Police Department. Bratton, a believer in the Broken Windows theory, decided to crack down on fare-beating and arrest the people who were cheating the system. He went after squeegee-wielding panhandlers and took on eradicating graffiti and litter.

His strategy worked. His methods were so successful that New York City experienced a 50 percent reduction in crime and a notable increase in cleanliness. The transformation has become legendary.

This argument for taking care of problems when they first arise is especially relevant to dealing with bullying behaviors immediately. When discipline is lax, it gives the message that you can torment your classmates with impunity.

THE LAW OF THE FEW

Pulling together Gladwell's three agents of change as a strategy to change
the school culture begins with the Law of the Few. It makes good sense to
gather a cadre of students who carry significant influence with their peers and
leverage their leadership.

Julie Dombo, a school counselor at a Haysville, Kansas, middle school created a Natural Helpers program in 1997 that trains 20 eighth grade students to
become role models and mentors to sixth grade students. The Natural Helpers
are nominated and selected by their peers in the spring of their seventh grade
year. One of their projects was conducting a pink shirt campaign. The concept
came from a report in Canada where a boy who wore a pink shirt to school
was razzed and called sexual names. The next day a whole group of boys
came to his defense by wearing pink shirts.

This program was kicked off in September by a school assembly where
Fried spoke and the Natural Helpers all wore pink t-shirts. They acted out
skits that demonstrated bullying situations and showed how the situations
could be solved by students. Fried worked with the Natural Helpers following the assembly and during the course of the year, the Natural Helpers
made themselves available to be good listeners and tutors, encourage positive
behavior, and defuse conflicts between students.

Testimony to their impact came halfway through the year when a group of
mean-spirited girls began bullying a girl who always wore a bow in her hair.
The intimidation came in many forms and kept increasing in public humiliation. One day the clique of hurtful girls came to school wearing bows in their
hair as a form of ridicule. The Natural Helpers inspiration served as stimulus
and through word of mouth, a small but highly visible number of students came
to school the next day wearing bows in their hair, including countless boys!
By the end of the day, as the idea caught on, more and more students found
ways to participate. Even teachers, both male and female, appeared with bows.
The clique of mean girls became quite contrite and their bullying stopped. Such
is the Law of the Few.

THE STICKINESS FACTOR

What messages can we convey to bullies, targets, and witnesses that will have
an impact? In the world of bullying, the Stickiness Factor has a strong connection to authentic stories.

The Student Empowerment Session (SES) qualifies for the Stickiness
Factor and it is detailed in Chapter Nine. That Session begins with the true
account of a young girl, named Kimberly Weisel, who was made fun of

by her classmates in elementary school when she became bald because of chemotherapy treatments. Students are deeply touched by the taunting she experienced, the pain she felt and always remember the "Kim Story."

At the end of a conversation, we tend to recall more of what we had to say than what others offered. When students actively participate in the lively SES discussion, the comments they make will stick with them but the most compelling part of the SES comes at the conclusion when many students are moved to apologize to classmates they have offended. Gladwell says that the Stickiness Factor has "to be memorable and move us to action."

THE POWER OF CONTEXT

What are the details to which we must be attentive? The Power of Context is illustrated by Mariner Middle School in the Lee County, Florida, School District. Statistics were collected on violence related incidents (VRI) from the time the new school opened its doors in the fall of 2004. VRI include battery, disruption, disrespect, fighting, gang related act, horseplay, insubordination, peer conflict, profanity, sexual harassment, threat/intimidation and weapons possession. In 2005–06 school year, the student population jumped from 782 students to 1292 students and the total VRI from 1,407 to 4,852. It is important to note that while the student population less than doubled, violence more than tripled (See figure 7.1).

Kathleen Saucier, a certified BullySafeUSA Trainer, became the school counselor in the fall of 2006. She began conducting student empowerment sessions, training the staff on bullying behaviors, working with parents, and serving as a counseling resource to hundreds of students who were dealing with countless personal and family problems.

She facilitated bullying prevention activities, focusing on relationships and respect, and secured grants from the local chamber of commerce to purchase copies of Stephen Covey's *Seven Habits of Highly Effective Teens* for her students.

Saucier dressed as a clown, brought laughter into her presentations, told stories, cajoled, and confronted her students. Verbal bullying was treated as seriously as physical bullying. She activated and empowered students to have a voice in the legislative process as the state moved forward to pass antibullying legislation. She contributed information on the school Web site and submitted articles in the newsletter that went to parents. Through it all, she was relentless about paying attention to the important little infractions. At the end of the 2006–07 school year, the total student population had leveled off at 977 and the VRI dropped to 1,386. There was a significant drop in every category. The largest decrease was in the area of disruption, from 2,982 to 666.

OFFENSE	SY0405	SY0506	SY0607
BAT	50	46	16
DIS	503	2982	666
DRS	381	192	117
FIT	58	141	62
GRA	0	9	5
HRS	82	243	110
INS	141	689	180
PRC	90	209	100
PRO	57	274	111
SXH	10	5	2
TRE	33	43	12
WPO	2	19	5
Total Incidents	1407	4852	1386
Total Student Pop	782	1292	977
BAT	Battery		
DIS	Disruption		
DRS	Disrespect		
FIT	Fighting		
GRA	Gang Related Act		
HRS	Horseplay		
INS	Insubordination		
PRC	Peer Conflict		
PRO	Profanity		
SXH	Sexual Harassment		
TRE	Threat/Intimidation		
WPO	Weapons Poss		

Figure 7.1.

Insubordination was reduced from 689 to 180, profanity from 274 to 111, and peer conflicts fell from 209 to 100. The Broken Windows theory was put in play by enforcing rules against profanity, insubordination, and disruption, along with battery, fighting, and weapons possession. Simultaneously, positive behaviors were rewarded and recognized.

The complete statistical information chart from Mariner Middle School is Figure 7.1. There are three sets of data—2004–05, first year of school; 2005–06, preintervention year; and 2006–07, the postintervention year.

PEER AND COMMUNITY INFLUENCE

Judith Harris, author of *The Nurture Assumption*, a rather controversial book, maintains that family influence is not always as important as we have been led to believe. She argues that peer influence, as well as community influence, are more significant in determining how children turn out. One of her most potent examples is that even when parents speak a foreign language at home, children are more inclined to use the language and accent of their peer group. Based on studies of juvenile delinquency and high school dropout rates, she posits that a child is better off in a good neighborhood and a troubled family than he or she is in a troubled neighborhood and a good family, which supports Gladwell's Power of Context concept.

What outcomes can we expect of a child from a troubled family, living in a troubled neighborhood, attending a troubled school? How much influence can a good school have in spite of a troubled neighborhood, where many troubled families live? Harris calls on us to keep our minds open to disturbing questions. We know there are many schools that serve as an anchor for our children when their family life is turbulent. Certainly, the influence of peers needs to be included as we challenge our thinking.

CHANGING THE CULTURE

In our travels we have come across wonderful people, doing innovative thinking—people who are looking at the bigger picture and expanding their concerns from problem solving into grappling with systemic change. These visionaries are incubating approaches that might very well become institutionalized at some point in the future.

Social Norming

A fairly new concept that is attracting considerable attention around the country focuses on changing social norms. Michael Hines and H. Wesley Perkins are credited with giving leadership to a grass roots movement called "social norming."

Social norming relies on solid information to challenge student misperceptions. The premise was used initially to curb drinking. Dr. James Turner, at the University of Virginia at Charlottesville, states that "perceptions of what your peers do are very, very powerful motivating factors. And misperceptions can be just as powerful." Through the use of surveys at the college, it was learned that the majority of students were making good choices when it came to alcohol consumption. By publicizing actual student norms instead of allowing misperceptions to be influential, drinking behavior changed. At colleges everywhere, alcohol-related deaths are on the rise, but at the University of Virginia no student has died from intoxication or an accident linked to drinking since 1998.

The social norms approach was then used successfully at many other colleges and high schools to reduce smoking, drinking and driving, and encourage the use of seat belts. Relating the social norm theory to bullying is a more recent step. The starting point is to give students credible data from their own school, rather than state or national averages.

At a National Social Norms Conference in July 2006, Perkins and Craig gave a specific example from a survey. In regard to reporting bullying to an adult, 74% of middle school students indicated that they should report bullying situations to adults, but 53% believed that their peers would not think it was the right thing to do. Sharing this kind of data with students could tip the reporting action.

While we are appalled at the numbers of children who are involved in bullying, there are many more who are not involved. Perhaps we can contribute to the social norm theory by surveying and publicizing the numbers of children who treat each other respectfully and choose to stand up for peers who need support.

Positive Behavior Interventions and Support

Positive Behavior Interventions and Support (PBIS) is another exciting initiative that began at the University of Oregon many years ago. The program stresses teaching the behaviors you expect from students, the same as you would with academic concepts. PBIS is not a set program, but something that is created by the administrators and teachers within their building,

At Blackhawk Middle School, in Bensenville, Illinois, the PBIS Team also included students. The team met over the summer and looked at behavior concerns from the previous school year. From this came the creation of a matrix of behavioral expectations—Be Safe, Be Respectful, and Be Ready. These words are found throughout the school building—the halls, every classroom, and in every student's assignment notebook. Every teacher implemented the Behavior Lesson Plans that were designed by the PBIS Team and discussed the desired behaviors to their students on the first day of classes. For example, under "Be Respectful," the behavior expectations include "Use positive and appropriate language" and "Be kind and polite to everyone." Reteaching and reminding continued throughout the year. As opposed to traditional approaches that focus only on undesired behaviors, PBIS stresses a constant recognition of compliance with the behavioral expectations. Every six weeks a Celebration of Good Behavior takes place during lunch for students who have honored the matrix with a limited number of office referrals and no suspensions.

An additional incentive is Blackhawk Bucks that are passed out by teachers to students who demonstrate exceptional behavior. The reward for accumulating Blackhawk Bucks includes VIP seating at assemblies, going to the front of the lunch line for a week, and even lunch with a staff member of their choosing.

Fried had worked with every grade level the previous year, conducting Student Empowerment Sessions, which focused on bullying reduction. In conjunction with the PBIS, if a student is bullying another student, a witness may say, "You're not using positive language" or "You're supposed to be kind and polite to everyone." According to Nicole Robinson, Blackhawk vice principal, in-school and out-of-school suspensions have dropped dramatically in the areas of bullying and fighting.

When we are successful in dramatically reducing bullying, we need to fill the vacuum with a positive force. If we don't, physics informs us that the negative behavior will rush back in to fill the space.

Saturation Effect

Years ago, Jay Winsten, Ph.D., Director of the Center for Health Communication, Harvard School of Public Health, came up with the concept of the designated driver, which has clearly changed the drinking and driving habits of millions of Americans. To accomplish that amazing change in social behavior, he orchestrated a "saturation effect" for Mothers Against Drunk Driving (MADD). There were national ad campaigns, articles in newspapers and journals, testimonials, and an easy to remember slogan—"Don't Drink and Drive." Winsten even persuaded writers of popular soap operas to use cocktail party scenes to script someone relinquishing their car keys when they had too much to drink.

A wonderful example on the current scene is Chrissa, an American Girl, Girl of the Year doll. There is no better way to reach countless young girls than with a popular doll who finds the courage to stand strong and speak out about bullying.

When Fried was a practicing dance therapist at several psychiatric hospitals in the Kansas City, Missouri, area she learned a valuable lesson from a patient, Brent, who had been an advertising executive prior to admitting himself for therapy. One morning, the movement therapy session focused on the subject of change. At the conclusion of the session, the group was discussing resistance to change, even when change is highly desired. As we pondered the contradiction, Brent offered to share something he had learned in "advertising school." He told us that marketing experts had done elaborate research to discover that it takes twenty-one contacts to convince a consumer to change their soap powder. If it takes twenty-one contacts to change attitudes about

ct, imagine how many contacts are required to change an ingrained
beha. or.

Replacing Bullying with Kindness

The saturation effect is exactly what Mary Jane Cole and her staff created at
Roosevelt Elementary School in Park Ridge, Illinois. Mary Jane Cole, principal, invited Fried to work with their students, staff, and parents. The next
year, Fried returned to conduct a BullySafeUSA Train the Trainer Institute
for counselors and other staff members from all of the elementary and middle
schools in the Park Ridge–Niles School District. The Institute was sponsored
by the Emotional Learning Foundation (ELF), a group of community citizens
who raise money to support innovative school projects throughout the school
district.

An outgrowth of that was the development of a Kindness Activities Program by staff from the Roosevelt Elementary School who participated in the
Training Institute. They pulled together activities from a curriculum guide,
"30 Activities for Getting Better at Getting Along," Fried and Lang, 2005,
from the magazine "*Teaching Tolerance*," a publication of the Southern
Poverty Law Center; a selected book list to support the activities developed
by the teachers, a collection of Kindness songs contributed by the school
music teacher; and a community service project where the Student Council
raised $5,000, matched by the PTO, for Operation Smile, a program that pro-
vides surgeries for children with cleft palates.

The students are introduced on a daily basis to positive messages of kindness and compassion, coming to them in a variety of engaging ways. Cole
says: "One thing to remember is that this district has an initiative to educate
the whole child, not just preparing them for high test scores but preparing
them to develop into caring and compassionate people.

Another kindness program that uses saturation was developed by a school
counselor, Jacque De Jesus, in the Blue Valley School District in Shawnee
Mission, Kansas. When you walk through the front door, you enter a magical
kingdom of kindness. There are pictures of students with their essays on kindness. There are strips of colored paper linked together in paper chains with
the names of students who have performed an act of kindness for someone in
the school. There are drawings and posters with kindness sayings everywhere
your eyes can take you.

Once a year, a contest is held and every student writes an essay about
his/her Kindest Kansas Citizen. Family members are not eligible. Each class
selects a winning essay and on a special Spring day, the Kindest Kansas
Citizens that were described are invited to attend a school assembly to listen

to the essay about them, read aloud by the student. The honored citizens have been teachers, neighbors, coaches, the school crossing guard, a physician, a soldier, and the school custodian, among others. Handkerchiefs absorb tears of joy. Every student essay that is written is mailed to the person they honored. What a glorious surprise to open the mail and discover that a student wrote an essay about you!

Another activity that leaped from the classroom to the adult world began when De Jesus presented a Kindness Seminar to all of the teachers in her building. Upon their return to their classrooms they were requested to speak to their students about kindness to each other, their parents, their siblings, their pets, and their environment and talk to them about how they felt when someone was kind to them and how they felt when they were kind to someone else.

Following that discussion, DeJesus instructed the teachers to be alert to a spontaneous act of kindness that a student performed. At such a moment, the teacher would place a special object, such as a red wooden apple, on the student's desk as a way of acknowledging his/her act of kindness. That student was then instructed to watch for another student's kind act and transfer the apple to *their* desk. What followed was remarkable! Teachers reported that students started overdosing on kindness because they wanted the apple on their desk. One teacher even recounted the day a boy dropped his pencil and four students dove to the floor to return it to its owner.

The culture in the classrooms and the entire school changed. When a group of us in the community, including Fried and Sosland, learned of this project, we decided that adults could benefit from this serial idea of kindness recognition.

We wear buttons that say "Kindness is Contagious, Catch it!" (created by artist Rita Blitt) or "Power of Kindness" (created by philanthropist Norman Polsky) and pass them on to someone we witness performing an act of kindness. It is very fulfilling to be able to honor such genuine gifts of the human spirit and we are always pleased by how meaningful it is to the person when we pass the button forward.

THE ART OF CREATING CHANGE

The status quo has tremendous advantage because "it exists, therefore it is." It has a history and it has advocates for its perpetuity. To alter the status quo we must first question current tenets, build support for their removal, and then have a compelling replacement plan at hand.

A crisis can be a boon to promote change. People are more inclined to question existing norms and take risks for change if a series of problems have surfaced. Fred Pryor, of Fred Pryor Seminars says that, "We are more inclined to risk the pain of change when the pain of staying the same is greater." We defined the crisis and the pain in Chapter One, when we identified health issues, truancy and dropout data, increase in youth suicides and crime, teacher shortages, and learning deficits. Increasing support for changing practices is coming from an awesome collection of people—educators and education policy makers, school counselors, school social workers, school psychologists, parent groups, legislators, the medical and mental health communities, law enforcement, national and international bullying prevention organizations, researchers, child advocates, the federal government, and the media. All are giving visibility and support for reexamining school practices. Home schooling and admissions to parochial and private schools are on the rise, giving additional evidence in the clamor for change.

Arne Duncan, a National Change Agent

Arne Duncan, who was appointed Secretary of Education by President Barack Obama, in 2009, has a vision for a radical change in our educational system. During a television interview with Charlie Rose, he spoke of schools being open from 9:00 a.m. to 9:00 p.m., seven days a week, 52 weeks a year. The schools would function from 9–3, and nonprofit groups would take over from 3–9, offering a full complement of after school programs, including drama, debate, chess, tutoring, sports, and mentoring. Literacy programs would be offered for adults, as well as GED courses.

He went on to share that every school has a library, a gym, and computer labs, which could be used by the community. Health services, including dental services, could be brought into the school environ, which would essentially become a community center. Duncan argues that society has changed and schools haven't caught up with the new norm. When Rose asked what it would take to make all this happen, Duncan replied, "A different mind set."

This twenty-first century mindset is not just a dream. Much of this happened in Chicago when Duncan was superintendent of schools, but there are other notable examples clearly showing that the idea is practical and possible.

The new mindset doesn't always start with educators. In the early 1990s, Bert Berkley, a Kansas City, Missouri, business leader, was asked by the Missouri Secretary of the Division of Family Services, Gary Stangler, to bring a business approach to the delivery of social services. The result was a citizen-based reform organization, named the Local Investment Commission (LINC).

As the group set about designing a one-stop resource base for children and families, they realized that schools were the logical setting. The group slowly began establishing what it called Caring Communities Sites in schools throughout the metropolitan area. Health, dental, and social services came together under one roof. An enlightened before and after school concept began in one school and grew to 75 within 6 years. The core value of the Caring Community Site is that local citizens must come together and design a plan that meets their neighborhood needs; LINC then helps make it happen!

The time is ripe for a different mindset, new thinking, and creative energy to change our culture. Our country is going through a cultural, moral, and financial tsunami, and a lot of people are in pain. What a perfect time to become a community of change agents.

Through countless contacts, connections, and conversations with passionate people who don't work in schools because it's a job but because they want to use their lives in the service of children and our future, we have collected a list of ideas that speak to creating a culture of caring. No single idea is a guarantee for change. It will require a combination of many concepts, a collaboration of many people to be the equivalent of installing a sewer system, and it will require individual change agents to become champions for the dream.

Our suggestions are not listed in order of importance but rather by the prospective sponsor of the idea. Some can be initiated by administrators, some by teachers, some by students, some by parents, some by policy makers, some by nonprofit groups, and some by members of the community. A truism, given to us by Mohandas Gandhi, prods us to "Be the change that you wish to see in the world."

As you read the ideas for our change agents in the next chapter, we hope you will be inspired to put as many ideas as feasible in place, to add your own ingenuity and to create a "Tipping Point."

Chapter 8

Change Agents

The greatest revenge is not to defeat the enemy but to change his heart.

—Author Unknown

This chapter provides a multitude of ideas from a multitude of sources. The Change Agents are listed under the titles of people best positioned to carry them out, not in any necessary order, and certainly not limited to these categories. Recognizing that many readers may have put a number of these concepts into action, this chapter serves to pique some fresh thoughts, inspire new ones of your own, and stimulate plans for partnership and collaboration with persons in your own system and the community. Originally parents were included as part of the Change Agents, but instead, a whole chapter has been devoted to their important role.

SCHOOL ADMINISTRATORS

The principal sets the tone for the entire school and is the most significant Change Agent. The values of the principal will influence every decision and can lift a school to extraordinary heights or condemn a school to a political battlefield.

Stake out your commitment to affect the culture of your school and to involve every single adult who has a presence in your building. Share your goal to engage students and parents in this exciting enterprise and appoint a task force to develop a comprehensive plan.

Staff training on effective bullying prevention and intervention techniques is a must. Having a shared vision by the administration, faculty, and nonteaching staff is the foundation for a school-wide approach. Make a special effort to receive input from cafeteria workers, custodians, bus drivers, and all other adults who have contact with students. They have extensive information about student behavior that is untapped.

Measure the success of your effort with a pretest and posttest instrument. The Mariner Middle School Instrument in Chapter Seven is an example. Conduct a climate survey with your students to determine their attitudes and observations about peer behavior. Be sure to phrase your questions to capture the "social norms" content found in Chapter Seven.

Define bullying as part of the school code of conduct. We recommend that physical, verbal, emotional, gender/sexual, and cyber bullying be specifically spelled out as unacceptable behaviors. Some schools have delineated very detailed rules and consequences for offenses. The more complicated the codes are, however, the less likely they are to be remembered. Principal Phil Hackett, of the Edwin Greene Elementary School in Cincinnati, Ohio, has had great success with the following conduct code—"Respect Yourself, Respect Others, Respect the Environment." The code is easy for everyone to memorize and all inappropriate behaviors fit into one of those commandments. Of course, all behaviors are closely monitored and enforced.

Many antibullying speakers, curriculum, and programs have proven their usefulness. Even the most powerful speaker requires follow through and continuous reinforcement. (See Chapter Twelve for resources.) Many schools will bring in a presentation as a kick-off to a year-long comprehensive commitment.

Make a very strong statement about your core beliefs at the entrance to your school. Hang pictures of heroes accompanied by their memorable sayings such as Einstein, Gandhi, Eleanor Roosevelt, and Martin Luther King, Jr., in the front hall. Posters and student art work that promotes peace making can be strong visual behavior reminders. Choose works that are substantive as well as decorative. The constant presence of these eye-catching prompts has an amazing capacity to affect students' attitudes.

Tap into character education programs that have been adopted all across the country. An exemplary resource is CHARACTER Plus, a division of the Cooperating School Districts of Greater St. Louis, that highlights a significant word of the month.

The program is a process rather than a curriculum and many schools have developed exciting ways to bring the word-of-the-month to life.

Use chants, affirmations, and or verbal rituals to begin each school day. At the Forrest Elementary School in Hampton, Virginia, Principal Kimberly Garvin-Richardson, begins the day with her students reciting a creed:

I WILL show respect to others, property, and myself.
I WILL accept responsibility for my actions.
I WILL listen to and follow directions.
I WILL use appropriate language.
I WILL do my best at all times.

This daily ritual is followed with a song—the Character Counts Pledge— that has been put to music by the school music teacher.

I pledge to be a kid of character, I will be worthy of trust.
I will be respectful and responsible, doing what I must.
I will always act with fairness, I will show that I care.
I will be a good citizen and always do my share.

Give playground supervision and recess options a high priority. Recess is one of the most frequently mentioned hot spots for bullying. When teachers are assigned to playground duty, it is essential that they spread themselves out and not cluster together. Playground supervisors and parent volunteers can make a tremendous difference. In spite of the concerns, recess has important benefits. Sacrificing play and downtime for more test preparation is not productive.

New research suggests that recess can influence behavior, concentration, and even grades. Romina M. Barros, a pediatrician and the lead researcher, claims that, "We should understand that kids need that break because the brain needs that break." In their study of 11,000 eight- and nine-year-old children, they found that those who had more than 15 minutes of recess a day showed better behavior in class than those who had little or none. Physical activity is especially important for young males.

In middle and high schools, insist that teachers stand in the halls between classrooms. Crowded hallways are ripe for cruelty. Awareness and supervision can make a tremendous difference for students at risk.

Cafeterias are another hot spot for bullying where supervision is required. Some principals take on the lunchroom duties so their teachers can have that precious time to be with their colleagues or have time for themselves.

Uniforms or some kind of uniform dress code are becoming more and more popular. Clothing issues, especially for girls, can be a horrendous source of taunting. Fashion trends, especially when students come from diverse economic backgrounds, can cause problems. Dress codes, such as solid color pants and white shirts can defuse a lot of issues. This type of uniform can instill a sense of pride while limiting ridicule. Many students have confided that they complained bitterly about the rule but were secretly thrilled to be relieved of the clothing competition.

Social and emotional learning for students have proven their worth. Programs that give children life skill training to make wise choices, sensible decisions, and function ethically not only turn out students who are good citizens they also increase academic achievement. An amazing study by Roger P. Weissberg and Joseph Durlak analyzed over 300 research studies and concluded that when social and emotional learning programs were offered, students ranked at least ten percentile points higher than their counterparts who were not involved in such programs. They also had better attendance records, were often less disruptive, and were less likely to be suspended.

Appreciate that bullies, especially at the elementary school level, are students with problems. Discipline must be enforced, but getting to the root of acting-out behavior is equally important. Every child needs at least one person who believes in him or her. When a parent is not that believer, someone else must step up to the role.

Stress witness training for students. Many school tragedies have been thwarted because student witnesses were privy to plans, threats, or bullying that they reported to authorities. Emphasize the importance of reporting information in confidence for the safety of everyone in school.

If possible, have an open door policy. A middle school principal in Baltimore, Maryland. announced that a jar of hard candies was on his desk, and students were always welcome to come to his office, obtain a piece of candy and stay for a brief visit. This was meant to encourage students to feel free to come to his office without being suspected of tattling or having gotten in trouble. This is especially important to increase reports by witnesses of bullying behavior.

Encourage community service and volunteer activities. There are so many ways in which students can begin to contribute and feel part of their community. Students who feel a sense of belonging and purpose are less likely to seek revenge for hurts. Be sure to make a connection between the community service project and life experience.

Don't pay special deference to athletes at the high school level. Sports "stars" need to adhere to the same rules and consequences as all other students. It is tragic to realize how many of our professional hero athletes have become corrupted and destroyed by the fame they couldn't handle.

Sexual language about gender orientation is rampant in middle and high schools. Confront the subject directly and reiterate that every child deserves to be safe in school—safe from physical, verbal, emotional, sexual, and cyber bullying attacks. When you describe how infractions will be handled, be sure to enforce the described discipline the first time one occurs—and every time thereafter.

Once you embark on a school-wide bullying prevention plan, all teachers must spell out the expectations and be consistent in dealing with infractions. If some educators follow the accepted plan and others don't, students will learn how to work the system and take advantage of any leniency.

Include art experiences—visual arts, plays, songs, dances, and musical productions. Proponents for Creative Expression programs cite numerous studies showing the value of arts in academic performance, sticking with tasks, school attendance, participation in math and science fairs, fewer court referrals, and better attitudes. For high school students, there is both a play and a video titled "Bang, Bang, You're Dead." It is incredibly powerful when performed by the high school drama department, and the video is extremely effective. (See Chapter Twelve.)

To change the culture will require the equivalent of a three-legged stool—the school, the students, and the parents. Inform all parents of your intentions to create a safe, caring, compassionate environment. Ask your PTA or PTO organization to host a meeting on the subject of school safety that includes a number of incentives—such as a spaghetti dinner, free baby-sitting services, and a "No-Homework" night. Use older students to help with babysitting and serving. Do not announce the meeting as a bullying program. Parents of the bullies and the witnesses will not attend and parents of the targets will attend with expectations of personal solutions. For those who do not attend, distribute a newsletter that outlines your plans, empha-size the vocabulary you will be using and the school code of conduct.

Create a power point presentation about your concerns, your goals, your activities, and some early successes. Make presentations to your local cham-ber of commerce, civic groups, and business leaders. Engage them and request contributions to fund specific aspects of your program—speakers, trainings, books, films, incentives, and so on. Contact your local newspaper to document your year-long program.

Become a champion for students in pain.

CLASSROOM TEACHERS

In some cases, a teacher can be an even greater influence than parents in a student's world. You may never receive the gratitude you deserve from someone whose life has been indelibly imprinted by your existence, but never doubt the power you have to change a life.

Institute classroom meetings every morning or several mornings a week at the elementary level. Creative teachers have put all kinds of special rituals in practice to ground students for the day; to instill manners and social etiquette, to resolve conflicts, and to teach children the art of giving and receiving compliments.

Many middle schools have daily home room meetings that can be used effectively to deal with peer relationship and behavior issues. If you are a Home Room teacher, especially for first year students, your classroom may be the very best opportunity to establish a trusting atmosphere where students can feel free to express the challenges of the middle school transition.

Humor is a winner! When students are asked to identify their favorite teacher, at any grade level, invariably it is someone who brings laughter to the classroom. If you tend to be on the serious side, consider the element of surprise and wear a clown nose one day, act out a lesson by changing your voice, throw in a joke or two, invite students to share a funny story, perform a magic trick to demonstrate a point. Be sure not to confuse humor with sarcasm.

Demand civility and courtesy and intervene immediately when inappropriate behaviors occur. Make this a priority at the beginning of the year and monitor consistently thereafter. Honor students who show respect, compassion, and kindness.

Include antibullying activities and exercises throughout the year. Changing behaviors and creating a sense of family requires constant reinforcement. Make your classroom a sanctuary of safety. Teach your students the concept of empathy. It should be a part of every student's understanding and behavior repertoire, yet many students are unfamiliar with the term. Use every opportunity to keep empathy alive and active with your classes. No bullying prevention program can succeed without empathy practice.

At faculty meetings, add social and emotional learning skills to the academic agenda. Decide on a focus for the week, such as no put-downs, a particular character trait and/or intentional acts of kindness.

Share personal stories of recovering from mistakes, lessons learned, and triumphing over difficult times. It is very meaningful to students to discover that teachers were on the receiving end of painful bullying experiences and channeled that experience into a teaching career.

Don't dismiss the quiet child who is not quick to raise his/her hand and participate in class discussions. The extroverted students will get lots of attention from other adults. Be the one person, perhaps, who recognizes the potential of someone who is often invisible to others but has a depth that hasn't been discovered.

Work at being fair and just with all of your students. It is normal to have preferences, but being "teacher's pet" can cause major problems for a favored child. Do not make comparisons with a student's sibling, for better or worse. Brothers and sisters can have entirely different personalities, capacities, motivations, and experiences in their family. Never humiliate or ridicule a student. Never allow a student to be humiliated or ridiculed in your class. Encourage students to report bullying situations and experiences to you. Assure them of your confidentiality and your desire to protect them from being in jeopardy. Talk to them about the difference between tattling and reporting.

If you lose your temper and behave in a way that you regret, apologize. Students need to see adults who take responsibility for their errors. Many parents never apologize for their mistakes and young people can benefit enormously from hearing and seeing a sincere, adult apology.

When you witness a colleague who is bullying students, take some constructive action. You would not want your own child to be in the classroom of a bullying teacher for an entire school year.

Establish a working partnership with the parents of your students. Try to develop empathy for an especially difficult parent, or at least their child. Dealing with parents of bullies who are in denial is a special challenge. We will deal more thoroughly with this issue and colleagues who bully in Chapter Ten.

Be sure to find ways to deal with your stress. Don't be too hard on yourself and take time to appreciate all that you give day after day after day.

If some of these ideas are of value to you, make a place for them in your lesson planning book so they will stay on your radar screen.

Become a champion for students in pain.

PHYSICAL EDUCATION INSTRUCTORS

Phys-ed or gym can be one of the most uncomfortable periods in the day for some students. Please do away with selecting captains and having them choose teams. Use a deck of cards to select teams or any other random, imaginative way you can think of. A parent comment: "The phys-ed instructors were always good at sports so they can't fathom what it's like to be picked last, day after day after day."

Check locker room behavior frequently. Keep students on their toes with your surprise visits.

Do not allow hazing activities to become part of an athletic ritual. Too many students have suffered severe emotional and sometimes physical experiences because of hazing. Students on the receiving end are supposed to "tough it up" and rarely report situations that have occurred until the consequences are severe. Be adamant about your disapproval of such activity.

Become a champion for students in pain.

SPECIAL EDUCATION TEACHERS

Bless you! You have one of the most demanding roles in the educational system. You have a special heart for children with special needs and you choose to share their survival journey.

However possible, find ways for your students to be treated with respect by their peer group. Work with the school nurse or the school counselor to make a special pitch about the difficulties that special ed students struggle with to all of the other classes. Enlist a pledge from all students to be supportive at best, indifferent at worst, but never to add additional burden to their daily challenges.

Discuss the different kinds of bullying that can occur and assure your students that they are not to blame when it happens. Talk about the best strategies to respond to their tormentors and have feedback sessions after they have tried out some of the ideas.

Have your students write some poems or essays about experiences they have with bullying situations that can be printed in the school newspaper. If there are some students who have been particularly helpful and kind, ask permission to include their names in the article.

Recruit some remarkable students to be a support group. Judy Bennet, an inclusion facilitator in the Shawnee Mission Kansas School District, organized a Circle of Friends for a special ed student, Stephen Rouse, who has Down's syndrome. She formed the group during their last year at elementary school to carry Stephen through the treacherous transition to middle school and the succeeding years. The group often met on weekends and after school. They went to movies, attended concerts, shared family vacations, and visited Stephen at his job. Stephen's parents were thrilled beyond measure when he graduated from high school with a B average and attended college away from home. Their appreciation for the Circle of Friends program is unbounded!

Become a champion for students in pain.

SCHOOL COUNSELORS, PSYCHOLOGISTS, SOCIAL WORKERS

You are an invaluable resource for your school principal because you have your finger on the pulse of the school. You have the unique capacity to be an advocate for students, for parents, for teachers, and other staff, and for programs and concepts that you have researched.

Use your skills to lead class discussions on bullying prevention. Consider offering the Student Empowerment Session for all the classes in your school as outlined in Chapter Nine. Determine a method to measure and evaluate the effectiveness of your program.

Arrange for staff training on bullying prevention and intervention, including special education and para-educators. Be sure to make the training available to nonteaching staff as well, such as school nurses, cafeteria workers, custodians, bus drivers, playground supervisors, parent volunteers, school secretaries, media specialists, school resource officers, crossing guards, and music and art teachers.

Put weekly memos in teachers' boxes with a bullying prevention idea. Recruit the artistic students, who are often on the fringes and rebuffed, to add graphics to the memos or to create cartoons on the topic.

Provide counseling for students who bully and are bullied. Do not bring them together to resolve a conflict unless the target requests such a session. Most targets will not feel comfortable divulging the extent of their abuse in the presence of their abuser.

When it is obvious that a student requires more intensive counseling than you can provide, take all necessary steps to see that such a student is referred for mental health care.

Research curriculum, videos, programs, speakers, books, and any materials that are effective tools for individual and group sessions. Identify best practices.

Offer empathy training sessions for every classroom and with all students. Organize peer helpers, peer mentors, and student support programs. Talk with older students in the school about reaching out to younger students. In middle school, match up sixth graders with responsible eighth graders as they begin this new experience. Discuss the risks and consequences of hazing.

Female bullying is especially vicious. Address this subject with girls at all age levels.

Numerous resources on this topic are available via the Internet. Most important is a frank, forthright discussion, facilitated by a skilled leader, such as yourself. There are some specific suggestions on this topic in Chapter Ten.

Match up every student who moves into your school with a trustworthy "buddy." New students are overwhelmed, some are grieving for the loss of familiar surroundings, and they are often rejected and excluded. They deserve a special welcoming process.

Become an advocate for bullying intervention and prevention in your school. Use all of your acquired skills to be persuasive with administrators who don't recognize the extent or consequences of bullying. Be a support to teachers who want to emphasize bullying prevention.

Conduct parent sessions on antibullying. Meet informally with parents of each grade level and explain the school's concerns, policies, and programs. Be prepared to deal with personal issues.

An astute counselor at one high school recruited and trained the top athletes to volunteer at a Children's Hospital. They had been treated so deferentially by students and staff, they became very full of themselves. She saw hospital service, where their athletic achievements were unknown, as a means to give them a different perspective on their reality.

Keep tabs on antibullying legislation and use your connections with your professional networks to support or oppose bills under consideration.

Become a champion for students in pain.

SCHOOL NURSES

You may be the first adult in the system to become aware of a student who is a target. Students who complain of stomachaches and headaches at recess time are giving signals of distress. Use their trust wisely when giving information to other staff.

At the beginning of the elementary school year, prepare a presentation on various health issues that students might be dealing with. In every classroom discuss hand washing, cancer, epilepsy, Tourette's, post surgery recovery, diabetes, ADD and ADHD, allergies, Asperger's syndrome, vision problems, asthma, children with disabilities, special needs, and any other diseases and illnesses that need to be brought to their attention. Talk about medications that students might need to take, i.e., Ritalin, insulin, etc., and how important it is not to make fun of someone on medication. Emphasize how fortunate students are who do not have to deal with health problems and how embarrassing and uncomfortable it is for students who are taunted because of matters they cannot control.

School nurses are frequently assigned to cover sexuality, puberty, and harassment. Become known as a resource in the system who is comfortable with this subject matter.

Have a private conversation with the parents of any students with health needs to see how you can be an advocate for their child in the system.

Share your knowledge and wisdom with administrators, counselors, and teachers.

Offer to be present at a parent conference with a teacher who needs support about a bullying situation.

Become a champion for students in pain.

BUS DRIVERS, CAFETERIA WORKERS, AND CUSTODIANS

Request an opportunity to be involved in any antibullying training sessions that take place. Insist that students treat you with respect and courtesy. Request that such courtesy become part of the Student Code of Conduct. Appreciate the special observations and information you have to offer.

Reach out to students whom you recognize are suffering. Because of your special role, you have unusual opportunities to offer support and caring.

Bus drivers have an awesome responsibility to maintain safety and order simultaneously. There are always some students who will take advantage of this dual role. Student passenger behavior can include shouting, tripping, screaming obscenities, throwing spitballs, shoving students against windows, terrorizing younger children, destroying homework, and sexual harassment. Do not allow bullying behavior of any kind on your bus, and make sure that you have the authority to expel disobedient students. More and more schools are installing surveillance cameras on school buses.

Ask for a specific staff liaison to receive reports of behavior issues, to receive information you overhear, and to deal with your concerns. When you make a report, ask to receive notification of any action taken. Suggest that all bus drivers meet on some regular basis with the staff liaison to provide feedback on bus behavior situations. When reports are made, become informed about any action taken.

When appropriate bus behavior becomes the norm at the very beginning of elementary school, it can prevent serious problems at the secondary level. When students are not responsive to rules, some bus drivers return to the school grounds until order prevails.

You are the first and the last contact of the school day. Use your twice a day connection to build a personal relationship with your passengers and their parents. Invite parents to come to the bus stop at the beginning of the year to become personally acquainted. A school district in Cincinnati has an open house at the bus depot before school begins. Parents and children are invited to attend and "Get to Know Your Bus Driver."

Some bus drivers have been known to discover the birthdays of every student on their bus route and create a birthday ritual. Do something special for students with summer birthdays.

Cafeteria workers can spot children with eating disorders and students who are caught in food and lunch money extortion. Share your valuable information with a staff liaison and ask to receive a report on action taken. A cafeteria worker observed a young girl who was only ordering a drink at lunch every day, reported it, and a case of anorexia was brought to attention.

Students on the free lunch program may need some extra tender loving care on a Monday morning after a rough weekend at home. Hugs and extra helpings of cinnamon rolls can feed famished souls as well as empty tummies. Cafeteria personnel can set the tone for the beginning of a new week.

Food service staff have been known to offer a "job" to lonely students who are dropped off at school very early.

Custodians see students from a slightly different angle. They are more likely to come in contact with students in the hallways, the cafeteria, locker rooms, and bathrooms. They have rescued students that get locked in their lockers and have been known to clean bathrooms when they know that bullies are going to enter the premises.

Request a staff liaison to work with regarding behavior information about students. Mopping floors, with your supervision, is a more effective punishment than suspensions for students who relish the freedom from school.

Use your role to protect targets whenever possible. Bathrooms can be very dangerous places. Remove vulgar statements scrawled on bathrooms walls as soon as possible and protect students from swirleys. Be on the lookout for students with wet hair.

Locker rooms are another site of torment and vandalism, where custodians can be watchful and intervene effectively.

In conversations with countless bus drivers, cafeteria workers, and custodians we have found them to be caring people who consistently reach out to kids with problems. Their skills, their observations, and their good hearts deserve appreciation and respect.

Offer to be interviewed by students as a way of personalizing your connection to them. Students will be interested in questions such as: "How long have you had your job? What do you like best about your job? What do you like least about your job? What is the funniest thing that has ever happened on your job? These interviews, with photos, should be printed in the school newspaper.

Become a champion for students in pain.

LIBRARIAN AND DIRECTOR OF MULTIMEDIA CENTER

Use your access to the Internet to identify resources that address peer cruelty, promote empathy, and inspire kindness for faculty and students.

Present a list of books for the PTA or PTO to purchase on the subjects of bullying, stereotypes, and racism for different age levels, genders, and cultures.

Organize a special table to display books on bullying subjects. Invite students to write reviews about books they read with specific recommendations for age and gender and to rate the books from one to four stars. Post several reviews for each book that is read.

At the end of the year, publish a list of the books with the most stars and recommendations they have received.

Make arrangements to have older students read books about bullying problems to younger students. Especially invite bullies to be readers. As the saying goes, "we learn by teaching."

Have students create unique bookmarks about bullying prevention. A student at Stephen Mack Middle School in Rockford, Illinois, came up with one that had the words STOP Problems, Anger, Insults, and Negativity (P A I N) on one side and BE Knowledgeable, Inclusive, Nicer, and Decent (K I N D) on the other.

Become a champion for students in pain.

MUSIC AND ART TEACHERS

Music and Art instructors bring a special touch to the development of the whole child. A study that followed some 25,000 students in 1,000 schools across the United States discovered that students who were involved in arts programs showed higher academic performance, had increased standardized test scores, had lower dropout rates, had fewer court referrals, had an increased ability to express anger appropriately, were three times more likely to win an award for school attendance, and other positive findings.

Use your art and music background to encourage empathy and kindness. "A Kindness Song" is attached to the end of this chapter (see figure 8.1).

Become a champion for students in pain.

PLAYGROUND SUPERVISORS

Because the playground is one of the most terrorizing haunts for bullies, it calls for unusual attention. Playground supervisors and the parent volunteers they supervise can make a tremendous difference. In addition to the overt expressions of physical and verbal abuse, playgrounds teem with examples of isolation and ostracizing.

One solution in use is a "Conversation Bench." An adult stands at the bench with a flag announcing that conversation is available. This is a great alternative for students who are often excluded or attacked during recess, without fear of being stigmatized. It is also beneficial for students with injuries and health issues.

A combination of unstructured and structured recess activities gives students a choice and relieves some of their concerns. Create a structured activity when you notice a number of children who are spending recess alone.

At Brooks Elementary School in Windsor, California, the PTA has arranged for an alternative recess. Every Friday, parent volunteers offer board games, bingo, bead stringing projects, knitting, and arts and crafts in a room set aside for this purpose. They thought their project would attract a small group of children, but out of 450 students who share recess, 125 flock to the Activity Room, and they have asked for the program to be extended to three days a week.

At Tillman Elementary School in Kirkwood, Missouri, they have two big rocks at the back of their playground that are used effectively to settle disputes. When a conflict occurs, students are directed to go to the Talking Rocks and "talk it out." A "Talking Tree" could work or some other playground landmark. Also at Tillman, Debbie Fechter, a staff member, takes photos of students who make good choices on the playground and other hot spot areas. Enlarged pictures of their smiling faces are displayed on the walls of the cafeteria all year.

Become a champion for students in pain.

SECRETARIES

Secretaries are the heart of operation central. Everything that happens in school radiates from the front office and defines the atmosphere of the school.

One of the most important roles is to serve as a buffer for the principal and vice principal(s). Secretaries can defuse angry parents by taking information and presenting it to the administrators before the call is returned.

Become familiar with custody issues to make sure that a parent who is not the legal guardian does not remove a child from school.

Be the cheerful spirit in the office that sets a warm, inviting tone for all who enter. Treat students who are sent to the office for discipline with respect.

Request a "petty cash fund" for students who forget to bring lunch money, field trip money, etc.

Never underestimate your capacity to be the "face" of the school and affect the school environment.

Become a champion for students in pain.

SCHOOL RESOURCE OFFICERS

School resource officers (SRO) serve as educators, role models, youth advocates, a law enforcement presence, and a liaison with the community. They
have wide latitude to listen and respond to children's needs, to deal with situations in a calm and effective manner, and to offer security.

Take on bullying prevention and intervention as a high priority and offer
to speak at parent and staff meetings. Inform students and parents about
bullying behaviors that violate the law and how they can be charged and
prosecuted.

Use your status to encourage exemplary behavior. An SRO at an elementary school in Salina, Kansas, Deputy Scott Thirkell started a special program
that recognizes students who have shown good citizenship, courtesy, kindness, and respect for others. Every two weeks, students are nominated by their
classroom teachers to be a part of "Officer Scott's Lunch Bunch." They are
seated at a table with a tablecloth and a special dessert. They also receive a
certificate and an enlarged picture of their lunch group.

Become a champion for students in pain.

SCHOOL CROSSING GUARDS

Crossing guards, along with bus drivers, are the first and last contact of
the school day for those children who walk to school. We have heard
heartwarming stories about these wonderful men and women who use their
role to make personal connections with students. Being greeted with a
smile and a wave that you can count on every day can smooth some rough
edges—coming and going. Every adult contact has the potential to lift the
spirit of a hurting child.

Become a champion for students in pain.

STUDENT ENGAGEMENT—WITH ADULT SUPPORT

Since students represent all three categories of bullying—bullies, targets, and
witnesses—no prevention program can succeed without involving students
directly in the implementation of a plan. Children, the same as adults, want
to be able to control their circumstances. Knowledge is power. Engaging students in the solution of concerns is a very effective course of action. Never
underestimate the wisdom that will come from involving them in conversations and discussions.

The Student Empowerment Session (See Chapter Nine) goes right to the core of student engagement. One counselor describes it as a "cleansing experience for the kids." Because it is presented in a generic way, it is nonthreatening. It is introduced as a teaching technique whereby students are educating adults about the breadth and depth of bullying. Students take the assignment seriously and it serves a double purpose, enlightening themselves and each other and educating adults. It is an extraordinary way to motivate students to become involved.

Witness training for all students is highly recommended. The adult community will never be in a position to observe all of the bullying activities that transpire. Witnesses need to feel empowered, confident, and safe to take some course of action. Witness training includes an understanding of the various ways that witnesses react to bullying scenes and options for constructive involvement. An activity that is part of the Student Empowerment Session (Chapter Nine) gives students a chance to consider high-risk vs. low-risk interventions. The activity also plants the seed for greater courage once they embark on the path to be a responsible witness.

An extensive array of peer mentoring and peer support programs exist. They operate under many different names, such as peer mentors, playground pals, befrienders, buddies, natural helpers, and peer helpers, and they have different priorities that include tutoring, emotional support, social inclusion, conflict resolution, and other goals. One constant is that the quality of the training and the supervision determines the effectiveness. Another universal element is the need to recruit a wide range of student leadership, not just the top of the ladder group. If gangs are a problem at your school, include some gang leaders.

Restorative justice is a fairly new concept that has a number of advantages over punishment and expulsion. James Wilson, author of *The Moral Sense* looks at three reasons people behave: level one—to avoid pain, level two—for respect or reward from one another, level three—for respect of self. Diane Gossen, author of *It's All About WE, Rethinking Discipline Using Restitution,* focuses on the latter. Instead of asking "Why didn't you do what you should have done?" Gossen asks: "How are you going to make things better?" "What's your plan to solve the problem?" "What kind of person do you want to be?" A preferable resolution for peer conflicts is for the bully to redeem him/herself through mutually agreed upon restitution.

Students are never too young to learn the value of giving to others. All students can benefit from making a contribution to their community. Volunteerism has proven to reduce the school dropout rate, to change the way young people feel about themselves, and to change the way others see them.

At Shawnee Mission Northwest High School in Kansas, Ron Poplau created a community service credit course for high school students. The program attracts over 300 students during the school year, five classes each day, limited to thirty-five participants per class. Students work in the community, interact with senior citizens and children, and raise funds for worthy causes.

Youth Volunteer Corps of America and Canada draws young people from diverse ethnic and socioeconomic backgrounds and involves them in community problem solving through structured volunteer service during the summer and school year. David Battey is the founder and executive director.

Appreciation for diversity is essential in today's cosmopolitan atmosphere. Students of all races, cultures, religions, and gender differences are sharing neighborhoods, sports activities, and classrooms. Schools are the perfect forum to transcend prejudices that might come from the home or the community. *Teaching Tolerance*, a publication of the Southern Poverty Law Center, is, once again, a rich source of materials and ideas on this topic for use in the classroom.

Camp Anytown, a Youth Leadership Institute, is an extraordinary program that transforms students' attitudes about their prejudices, stereotypes, and biases. The National Conference for Community and Justice (NCCJ) sponsors this remarkable experience for high school–aged young people all across the country. An informative, in-depth evaluation of the program in the Kansas City, Missouri, area has been conducted by Walter T. Boulden.

In many schools, students of different races sit separately in the cafeteria. There are other divisions in the cafeteria that perpetuate student alienation. Sponsor a Mix-It-Up at Lunch Day once a month and spread the word that students are to sit at different tables, with different students than they usually join for lunch. Train some student leaders to facilitate a conversation and/or have young people sit at tables of their birthday month. Print out signs with the popular astrological qualities to encourage discussion.

Organize a panel of students with different cultural backgrounds to speak to social studies classes at the middle and high school level. Panel members should prepare a five-minute presentation and be prepared for a question and answer period to follow.

Using art and drama classes, engage students in designing antibullying and positive behavior posters and performing skits that illustrate typical disrespectful behaviors with a revision on the rerun. Integrating the skits with willing teachers in the role of the bullies can have a "stickiness" factor, especially when the bullies get their "comeuppance."

Appoint a student task force on cyber bullying at the middle and high school levels. The agenda could include the publication of a researched article in the school newspaper, a student definition of cyber bullying to be included in the code of conduct, a student's bill of rights regarding freedom from cyber bullying, presentations to the state legislature regarding protection of students from cyber bullying, a cyber bullying pledge to be signed by all students, and any other ideas that develop from the task force.

Many schools have instituted a box where students can deposit anonymous tips about bullying that is happening to themselves or others. Place a box where students can nominate champions of change right next to the tips box, so if a student is seen approaching the boxes, it would be hard to determine his/her intent. The box needs to be secured to guarantee confidentiality. The designated adult who is assigned to deal with the tips and the champs must handle the situations with discretion. An anonymous tips phone line can be installed, in addition or instead. The rules governing the tips box, the champions box and the tips line should be clearly explained to all students. Honor the champions of change who are nominated by their peers.

Call together a group of trustworthy students, ask for volunteers and invite champions of change to become members of a team to create a social norm of kindness and compassion in your school. Explain the Law of the Few and the power of even a few students to make a noticeable change in the school environment. Ask them to create opportunities for inclusion for students who have been rejected. One creative example of this strategy was a high school prom queen who invited a male student to dance with her at the prom. His status as an isolate was reversed and he claimed it was life-changing.

Become a champion for students in pain.

COMMUNITY

Every citizen is part of an energy imprint in our society. When a lot of angry people dump their hostility into a community, it infects our atmosphere. When people are intentionally kind and compassionate, something amazing can happen.

Much too often, young people are dismissed and disregarded by elders as troublesome. What would it take for all adults to look every child in the eye, smile, and greet them favorably, whenever they come in contact? What if we used our tone of voice and our body language to send out messages of respect for people of all ages?

Change agents even work in prison. Members of an inmate self-help program, Reaching Out From Within, in seven Kansas correctional facilities, meet weekly and recite a pledge of nonviolence. They work on managing their anger and treat their fellow convicts with respect. Their calmer behavior has an effect on others and the recidivism rate for the Reaching Out From Within members is 10.9 percent as compared to a national recidivism rate of over 60 percent.

"Dissing" is an underlying cause of a great deal of violence. A contest for a catchy slogan could be held. For example, "When I get dissed, I use my fist. When I'm respected, I act as expected."

An awesome example of a community change agent is Sue Head, executive director, Keeter Center for Character Education at College of the Ozarks, Branson, Missouri.

Sue was asked by the chancellor of her college to put a major emphasis on character. She took that one sentence assignment and initiated an extraordinary journey for her community. She began with the belief that people really want to be engaged, they want to make the culture safer, fairer, and better for everyone but are conditioned to wait for someone else to take responsibility.

Information had been released about the high rate of discipline issues in the schools. The first reaction from the community was to demand that the school administration do something about the problem! Sue's reaction was that teachers and the administration are being expected to do the impossible. "We are on the same team," she said. "We can't put another rock in the backpack of another teacher to climb a very steep hill!" Sue felt that students needed to be getting the message about their behavior from *everyone*—the YMCA, the dentist, McDonalds, the bus driver, at home, and at Sunday schools. She reasoned that nobody cares as much about our community as we do, and when we link arms together, that is our greatest strength.

Coincidentally, she attended a Character Plus Conference and heard Joan Davis speak about the character education concept where the community gets to decide the traits they want to embrace. Sue had been looking for a tangible way to get everyone involved.

She returned to Branson and invited anyone who would listen to her to become a First PLACE Partner. PLACE stood for Partners Linking Arms for Character Education. It didn't cost any money, there was no product to buy, the requirement to be a partner was to sign up and give contact information. She met with every organization, agency, and individual she could find and ended up with 1,000 names in a database.

The character education project recommended that the community be brought together to choose a "word of the month," which would promote good character. A town hall meeting was held to select the words. Attendees ranged from high school students to retirees. Fifteen character traits were placed on a ballot and the assembled group could vote for nine words—one for each month of the school year. People came to the microphone and passionately defended the word they felt best represented their community.

The outcome was September—Respect, October—Responsibility, November—Citizenship, December—Compassion, January—commitment, February—Honesty, April—Perseverance, May—Self-discipline. Each word had a connection to a particular month. By the end of the evening, the people decided they wanted to continue during the summer so they added June—Patience, July—Patriotism, and August—Courage.

She sent word out to everyone in her database to find a way to be *intentional* about demonstrating the trait of the month. The results were astounding! A local construction company painted the words: Get Mixed Up With First PLACE in big black letters on the side of their yellow concrete mixing truck. Realtors created yard signs with the trait of the month. The word was printed on McDonalds receipts, utility bills, and bank teller's windows. The local newspaper ran a full page in color every month, listing all of the First PLACE Partners. The list grew to 550! A radio station featured a different school every month with the activities they were doing to celebrate the designated word.

Sue would deny that she is a change agent. She believes that the community was waiting for a catalyst to energize their spirit and that *every* community is poised to do the same. Branson discovered that when character becomes imbedded in the community culture and reinforced in the schools, more teaching goes on, math scores go up, and attendance increases. The ultimate testimonial came from a school administrator who reported that his disciplinary rate was down as much as 50%. The goal had come full circle.

Sue reports that the community went on to tackle even greater challenges. When the economic crisis devastated Branson's tourism industry and many people lost their jobs, teachers were sending food home with students in their backpacks to get them through the weekend. The community is still linking arms to solve problems, this time dealing with poverty and hunger. As a result of another town hall meeting, 1400 volunteers served 8,000 people for dinner for 70 days—and the response continues as this is being written.

Become a champion for students in pain.

POLICY MAKERS

Thirty-eight states have passed antibullying legislation. Check to see if your state has such a law in place. If your state does have legislation, check with www.BullyPolice.org to see how your legislation is rated. Some states rank very high and Delaware has an A++ rating. See how your bill compares and work with legislators to bring your state bill to the highest standards.

If your state does not have legislation on this subject, BullyPolice will help you strategize. In Kansas, we found that bringing young people to testify was very persuasive. Children telling their authentic stories will be highly effective advocates.

Many bills have good language but lack accountability and funding components. Collaborate with your state department of education to conduct an anonymous survey where school districts will be honest about the extent of planning, training, staffing, and programming they are actually sponsoring, in the face of an unfunded mandate.

Cyber bullying has been a controversial element of antibullying legislation in some states. It has been opposed in some areas because it holds the school responsible for situations away from school property. Freedom of speech issues have been raised as well. When it has been included, the reasoning has been that the effects spill over into school behaviors and academics.

Gender orientation has also been a source of controversy. Sexual language has been tied to a number of school shootings and cannot be ignored. Some bills define the particular issues for targets that need to be protected. Other bills focus on the bullying without specifying types of children that are at greater risk. No conflicts regarding wording should be a barrier to ensure that *all* schools must be safe for *all* children.

Imagine a school where the administration has a clear vision of how to create a culture of compassion, caring, and citizenship that is a profound foundation for academic and personal success. Envision a school where teachers spend their time challenging eager minds, inspiring creativity, preparing young people for productive futures, freed from time-consuming discipline enforcement. Picture a school where students treat each other with respect, encourage each other to learn, experience kindness and empathy, and interactions do not lead to pain, rage, and revenge.

What if administrators, teachers, counselors, nonteaching staff, parents, and students shared the same vision and created a tipping point in their school? It can happen when change agents bring their passion to the dream and everyone becomes a champion for students in pain.

Chapter 8

THE KINDNESS SONG

Words: SuEllen Fried
Music: SuEllen Fried,
Gary Adams

Figure 8.1a.

Figure 8.1b.

Chapter 9

Engaging Students in the Solution

> I thought this was going to be one more boring lecture about bullying and
> I didn't want to be here. I can't believe what happened!
>
> —Steven, a student

The core component of the BullySafeUSA program, founded in 2001 by
SuEllen Fried is the Student Empowerment Session (SES). The session consists of a series of questions, in a particular order, for students K–12, which
have been tested over many years. There are variations for using the material,
depending on the age level of the children.

Fried has trained over 500 counselors, as well as health educators, teachers,
child advocates and parents, to conduct this SES. The training process requires
three days, which begins with an observation of Fried conducting the SES.
It concludes on the third day with the participants facilitating their own SES
with a group of students they do not know and observing a fellow participant
facilitate a comparable session. Participants become committed to this concept
of engaging children in a powerful dialogue because of its unique, effective
approach to capture their interest and their collective wisdom

To become a Certified BullySafeUSATrainer, it is necessary to participate
in one of the three day BullySafeUSA Training Institutes and then facilitate
the Student Empowerment Session with students for at least two consecutive
years. Following that time period, the potential trainer must be observed by
Fried, or a certified trainer for final accreditation.

The SES has been evaluated by Andrew Terranova, Ph.D., assistant professor, Department of Psychology, Stephen F. Austin State University, Nacogdoches, Texas. The evaluation is at the conclusion of this chapter.

Fried prefers to train school counselors for certification because they work with
a variety of grade levels and develop their expertise with students of different age

levels. As counselors, they are constantly on the lookout for research, films, videos, books, and other programs to round out their repertoire as they work with bullying and other student behavior issues. One of her certified trainers is a Second Step Trainer and another is a Certified Olweus Trainer. The BullySafeUSA program can be used in conjunction with other programs and/or approaches.

Prior to the publication of this book, the SES has never been made available without going through the training program. Understandably, a major concern is maintaining the quality of the delivery. Consequently, there are certain caveats that must be followed for the program to be effective.

THE SOCRATIC METHOD OF USING QUESTIONS AS THE PROCESS IS ABSOLUTELY ESSENTIAL

It requires a role reversal where you, the facilitator, become the student and the students are expected to be your teachers. This is not a gambit. Students have a fund of information to divulge and you will become all the wiser when you take the time to listen to them. If you are not comfortable relinquishing your authority to conduct this session, it would not be wise to attempt this SES. The institutes I have conducted usually have waiting lists of people who want to attend. On the one occasion, however, when administrators, teachers, and/or athletic coaches were assigned by their principal to go through this training, many acknowledged that this SES did not suit their style of student interaction.

ALL QUESTIONS SHOULD BE OPEN-ENDED AND ALLOW FOR A MULTITUDE OF ANSWERS

This material is not presented as a test with students being rewarded for the correct answer. Every response is to be treated with respect. It is important to find a way to honor every reply. For instance, if a student gives a definition of emotional abuse when you ask for an example of verbal abuse, respond by saying: "That is going to come up when we talk about emotional abuse so be sure to raise your hand again."

NEVER ALLOW STUDENTS TO RIDICULE ANY RESPONSE BY A FELLOW STUDENT

The integrity of the program depends on making the session a safe, bully-free experience. If any bullying should occur, it should be used as a teachable moment. Humor can be a valuable tool to ease situations. Once verbal bullying has been defined, you can remind the students that put-downs, name-calling, snickering, etc., are forms of bullying and are not permitted.

STUDENT EMPOWERMENT SESSION ADVANCE PREPARATION

- It is best to work each session with children at the same grade level, i.e., all of the fourth grade classes in a school together.
- The ideal number of students to work with is 40–60. This program has been used successfully with as few as 20 and as many as 250. The larger the number of students, the more difficult it is to make personal, eye to eye contact with every student and to bring the session to the conclusion that we seek.
- An intimate space, such as a classroom, the library, a music room or even the stage of the auditorium, is preferable to the cafeteria, the auditorium, or the gymnasium. The latter three present many challenges.
- Request one hour for the session at the elementary level—third through sixth. Forty to forty-five minutes is adequate for K–2 grades. Middle schools have a daily schedule that must be respected, usually forty-three to forty-seven minutes.

The same is true of high schools. Occasionally, a middle school principal will make the SES a high priority and arrange for an extended period of time. For grades K–2, I show a video, *Stop Teasing Me!,* which can be ordered from Sunburst. (See Resources, Chapter Twelve.)

- Every student needs to wear a name tag with his/her first name only, printed in big, black letters. This must be specified or you may see pink and orange scrawled names that are unreadable.
- If you must work in a gymnasium, cafeteria, or auditorium, ask for a hand microphone that will allow you to move around the area.
- A school psychologist or counselor should be present for the sessions. Students might reveal personal data that should be followed up by school personnel.
- If a student discloses personal data that involves child abuse, a report must be made to someone in authority before leaving the school.
- The teachers of every class should be present during the SES, but out of view. When the session takes place in the classroom, teachers should not use the computer or grade papers during the session. Encourage them to listen carefully to their students' input.

- You will need paper or a blackboard and writing materials. There are a number of words and figures that you will want to be visible, such as the five kinds of bullying.
- It will not be possible to go through this entire sequence, allowing major time for student responses, in one hour, much less in 43 minutes. I adapt each session to the needs of the particular group and determine spontaneously what needs to be eliminated, but this material includes the complete series of questions and demonstrations that I have used.
- Keep in mind that all children have developed in their particular environment and circumstances. If we could catch a glimpse of that context, we might have great admiration for their ability to endure, for their resourcefulness to meet their needs, and for their perseverance in the face of extraordinary obstacles.

STUDENT EMPOWERMENT SESSION

"Good morning, everyone. My name is SuEllen Fried." (Write your name on the blackboard or newsprint.) "I am delighted to be with you and to have the opportunity to gather a lot of information from you. Most of the time we spend together, I will be asking you questions and I need you to be as honest and open as possible. To make sure that we have lots of participation without things getting out of hand, tell me what signal I should use to quiet things down. Thank You.

"When I ask a question and you raise your hand to give an answer, please correct me if I mispronounce your name. Names are very special and I want to honor yours.

"Here's my first question—how many of you have every heard of child abuse?" (Most hands will go up.) "Who can tell me what child abuse is?" (Accept a few answers.) "You might be interested to know that when I was your age, the term child abuse didn't exist.

"For centuries, our society believed that children were the property of their parents who could do anything they wanted to with their offspring.

"In the 1970s we finally began passing laws to protect children but every child abuse law in this country specifies that abuse only occurs when the abuser is an adult. I believe that if a child is hurting, it doesn't matter if the person who is causing the pain is their parent or their classmate. If a child is suffering, it doesn't matter if the perpetrator is 35 or 10. I believe that bullying is a form of child abuse and no child deserves to be abused by anyone.

"Before I ask you any more questions, I want to apologize in advance because I am not going to be able to call on everyone who raises their hand for every question but I will do my best to call on everyone at some time during the session.

"The reason I am so concerned about bullying is because many years ago, I met a little girl named Kimberly Weisel. Kim was diagnosed with cancer when she was seven. How many of you know someone who has had cancer?" (Many hands will go up.) "Who can tell me what happens if you get cancer and you have chemotherapy?" (Someone will know that chemo causes your hair to fall out.) "That's a very important part of this story.

"Kim had chemo when she was seven and recovered but when she was ten, the cancer came back full force and the doctors decided that the best chance to save Kim's life was to have her spend her entire summer vacation in the hospital getting massive doses of chemo. I met Kim through my daughter, Paula, who worked at the hospital. Kim and Paula became very good friends and at the end of the summer, they knew that Kim was not going to survive. Paula suggested that we invite Kim and her mom to come to our house for lunch to celebrate their friendship before they went back to their respective schools.

"While we were visiting and chatting, Paula asked Kim if she was looking forward to returning to school. Kim said: 'I can't wait for school to start! I haven't seen any of my friends all summer.' Then Paula asked Kim if she had any concerns about going back to school. Kim thought for a moment and said: 'Recess.' 'Why recess?' I asked. Kim explained that at recess there were some children who thought it was fun to pull her wig off of her head. When that happened, other children formed a circle around her and started pointing and laughing at her.

"I have never recovered from that conversation. I have never been able to put out of my mind a ten year old girl who was trying to figure out a way to let go of her life, her family and her friends—and her biggest problem was peers at recess who thought it was amusing to make fun of her because she was bald because of cancer treatments.

"If students at Kim's school could be that cruel, I began to wonder if there were other schools where bullying was happening. I started going to schools and asking students, 'What are you doing to each other, why are you doing it, and what could we do to make it different?'

"One of the things I have learned is that there are five kinds of bullying—physical, verbal, emotional, sexual, and cyber bullying." (I do not include sexual bullying until the fourth grade. If third grade students bring the subject up, accept their response. Some facilitators prefer to use the term *gender* bullying instead of *sexual* bullying.)

"What is physical bullying?"

(Students will offer examples—kicking, hitting, punching, any body contact, etc. See chapter 4.)

"What is verbal bullying? Before you give examples, please complete the following sentence—sticks and stones can break your bones but. . . ." (Students will reply with "names can never hurt you.")

"Do you think that is true?" (Students will say, "No.")

"I would like to teach you a new sentence. Sticks and stones can break your bones but words can break your heart. Please say that with me." (Students repeat.) "Who has had a broken bone?" (Hands go up.) "How long did it take your broken bone to heal?" (This is a good opportunity to call on someone who hasn't participated, but you won't have time to call on everyone.)

"Broken bones can take a few weeks, a few months, sometimes a year to heal. How long does it take to heal a broken heart?" (Students will reply, "Never," or "Forever.")

"Now tell me, what is verbal bullying?" (Students will give examples—name-calling, put downs, etc. See Chapter Four. If *gossip, spreading rumors, betraying a secret* are not mentioned, be sure to state those examples.)

"What is emotional bullying? Give me examples of bullying where there is no physical contact and no words are spoken." (Students will offer examples—rolling your eyes, sending notes, using the third finger, body language, etc.; see Chapter Four. If *excluding someone* is not mentioned, be sure to talk about leaving someone out, not letting someone sit next to you on the bus, rejecting and isolating. If you have time, tell the story of the birthday party when no one came.)

"What is sexual bullying?" (Students will give examples of touching someone where they shouldn't be touched, making fun of someone's body, etc.; see Chapter Four. This is uncomfortable for many students, so acknowledge that this is a squirmy subject but very important to discuss. If students are still reluctant, mention examples that you have learned from other students. Sexual language *must* be discussed.)

"There is a form of sexual bullying that we need to discuss—sexual language—using words like gay, queer, homo, you know what I'm talking about, don't you?"

(Heads will nod.) " The reason I am willing to stand here and say these words is that many of the school shootings happened because of those words. Boys in prison who committed murders have told interviewers that being called those words, over and over, pushed them over the edge. I plead with you to give up this lethal language. I do not want to read about one more student who has been killed by a classmate because of sexual words."

"What is cyber bullying?" (Students will give examples, saying mean things about someone in a chat room, stealing someone's password, putting stuff on MySpace, etc., see Chapter Four.) "It is so cowardly and so cruel to torment someone anonymously and then send the messages to untold numbers. Targets have no way to defend themselves against such widespread mean communication. You need to know that technology has been developed to track down the senders of such messages and cyber bullies will not be exempt from discovery.

"Now, I want you to vote on which form of bullying you feel is most common at your school. Physical? (take vote) Verbal? (take vote) Emotional? (take vote) Sexual? (take vote) Cyber bullying?" (take vote).

(Physical bullying gets few or no votes. Fights are obvious and intervention occurs almost immediately. That is not the case with verbal bullying, which invariably receives the most votes. Emotional bullying receives a sprinkling amount of votes from students, but receives the most votes from teachers and adults who are present during the session. Sexual bullying and cyber bullying also receive a smattering of votes, but something changes dramatically when the next question is posed.)

"Which kind of bullying do you think causes the most stress or concern for targets?"

(There has been a consistent vote all across the country by students for sexual bullying. Middle school students have always identified sexual bullying as a major issue, but in the last several years, even fourth, fifth, and sixth graders are casting their votes for sexual bullying. More recently, however, votes for cyber bullying, especially among middle school students, have increased).

"Bullying causes pain and I want to share something I've learned. I'm going to draw this on the board for you." (Draw PAIN, RAGE, REVENGE cycle from Chapter One).

Pain doesn't evaporate, it doesn't disappear. It collects, and when enough pain collects, it turns to Rage. And then the Rage can become Revenge. Revenge causes Pain and the cycle starts all over again! This cycle doesn't happen just happen in schools, it happens between religions and tribes and countries and becomes a global problem. We must stop pain, wherever and whenever we see it if we want to make the world a peaceful planet."

(Draw the PAIN, DEPRESSION, SUICIDE cycle from Chapter One on the board). "A boy came up to me after a session like this and he told me that I needed to draw another cycle—Pain, Depression, and Suicide. He told me that when he is in pain, he doesn't become aggressive, he becomes Depressed, and when he gets Depressed he starts thinking about Suicide. He told me that the only reason he hasn't committed suicide is because of the pain it would cause his parents."

(Draw third cycle on the board—the one that is the combination of the first two from Chapter One). "Months later, a young boy observed my two drawings, and told me that I needed to figure out a different drawing—one that combined the two. He told me that some days he wakes up and wants to get even with everyone who has tormented him and the next day he just wants to stay in bed, pull the covers over his head, and think about doing away with himself. Please do everything you can to stop pain."

"We need to talk about targets, bullies, and witnesses. I am very concerned about targets." (Write the word "targets" on the blackboard.) "One hundred and sixty thousand children stay home from school every day because they are afraid of what might happen to them on the bus, the playground, the cafeteria, the bathrooms. There are more and more students who are showing up in doctor's offices with headaches and stomachaches and depression because of the way they are being treated by their classmates. There are students who are committing suicide because of bullying. There is even a new word that describes this action and it will probably end up in the next edition of the dictionary. The word is *bullycide*."

"I am also concerned about bullies." (Write the word "bullies" on the blackboard.) "Over 30 years ago, a very wise researcher by the name of Dr. Leonard Eron was concerned about bullying. He persuaded a school district that had 875 students in the third grade to allow him to conduct a survey. They printed out the names of every third grade student and then asked every student to take a pencil and put a check mark in front of the name of every student they thought was a bully. All the students made their check marks, the papers were collected and put away in a filing cabinet for 10 years.

"When the third graders became seniors, the process was repeated. All the names of the seniors were printed out and the students were asked to make a check mark in front of the name of any student they considered to be a bully. When the researchers compared the two lists, they learned that almost every senior who received a check mark, had received a check mark when they were in the third grade. Nothing had changed in ten years.

"The researchers were curious to see what was going to happen to those bullies when they became adults so they waited ten more years and found a significant number of the people who had been identified as bullies when they were in school. What they discovered was that *one* out of every *four* bullies checked on the survey, had a criminal record by the time they reached 30 years of age. The males were more likely to become men who abused their wives and the females were at greater risk to become mothers who abused their own children. Bullies not only hurt other people, they hurt themselves as well.

"Witnesses are the key to the solution of bullying. (Write the word "witnesses") on the board and circle it.) How many of you have seen some of the law shows on TV? Then you know that a witness is someone who sees what happens and has to tell the truth. Here's another study. Researchers went into a school and asked the teachers how frequently they intervened in bullying situations. Seventy-one percent of teachers say they almost always intervene in bullying situations. When the students were asked about teacher intervention, they reported that teachers intervene only 25 percent of the time. We think the difference in the perception is not that teachers don't *care* it's that they aren't *there*. But witnesses, you are there!

"Because you are there, we need you to get involved. I need seven volunteers to help me with an exercise about witnesses." (Hand each of the seven students a card and ask them to form a line in front of the class. Each card contains a different statement: TELL AN ADULT, DON'T GIVE BULLIES POWER, INCLUDE A TARGET IN YOUR ACTIVITIES, CHALLENGE THE BULLY, BEFRIEND A TROUBLED BULLY, SUPPORT A TARGET IN PRIVATE, GET A GROUP TO CHALLENGE THE BULLY.)

"These are actions you could take as a witness. Please read all of them and tell me which one is the most risky." (Challenge the bully is invariably mentioned as the riskiest.) "Will the person with 'challenge the bully' please move to the front of the line? What is the next riskiest?" (Continue asking students to tell which is the next riskiest until all seven students have moved to places in the order of most to least risky. The middle five will vary each time but 'support a target in private' usually ends up as the least risky. Affirm all responses.) "Thank you very much. Challenging the bully can be very risky. I'm not asking you to do anything that makes you uncomfortable, but there is one thing that everyone of you can do and it's very important. Talk to a target when no one else is around." (Ask for a student to volunteer to be a target. Turn to that student and say the following words: 'You don't deserve to be treated this way. I'm so sorry I can't make it stop'. Ask the student to share with the class how it felt to hear those words. The student will confirm how much it means hear that someone else is aware of what is happening and believes that it is wrong.)

"Some students have told me that they wanted to report what was happening to an adult, but they were afraid they would be accused of being a snitch or a tattletale." (Write "tattling" and "reporting" on the board. Ask students to tell what the difference is. Accept all answers and if it hasn't been given report the following.) "Many students have said that tattling is when you are

trying to get someone IN trouble" (draw an arrow going down) "and reporting is when you are trying to get someone OUT of trouble." (Draw an arrow
going up.)

"Here's an important question. Why does someone become a bully?"

(Students will say: "'Bullies have problems in their family, they're being
abused at home, an older brother or sister is picking on them, they want
revenge, they need attention, they want to be popular, they're bored, they're
mean and nobody makes them stop, they've seen something on TV or on
video games and they're copying it, they don't know how to handle their
anger, they can get away with it, they're scared inside and they don't want
others to know it so they act tough, maybe someone in their family has died
or is very sick or their parents are getting a divorce and they can't handle the
pain, they don't feel good about themselves so they want others to suffer,
they think it's cool, they're jealous, they have a 'crush' on someone and pick
on them to get their attention, they don't have self esteem, they want power,
their parents never taught them what was right and what was wrong, they're
involved with drugs or alcohol, or bullies want to control everybody else
because they can't control themselves").

"Your comments are extremely insightful. You are saying that bullies are
very troubled, that they are needy and have lots of problems.

"This is a good time to share a story with you about a group of fish. This
story comes from a book by Dr. Karl Menninger, *The Human Mind*. Dr. Karl
told about a group of fish who were swimming in a pond. The came upon
a fish who was upside down and it was flapping its tail. The group of fish
thought that was really weird so they swam away from the flapping fish as
quickly as they could.

"The reason the fish was upside down and flapping its tail was because it had
a hook in its mouth and it was doing the best thing it could do. Dr. Karl went
on to say that there are a lot of people who have hooks in their mouths that are
invisible to us and if we could see their hook, we might appreciate that they are
doing the best they can, considering the circumstances that they are in."

"I want to talk with you about why someone becomes a target. Usually
students will say because they are *different,* so over the years I have collected
a list of *differentnesses.*

"Because you're too tall, too short, too heavy, too thin, too rich, too poor,
too smart, too slow, different color hair or skin, or religion or culture, just
moved from another school, wear glasses, have braces, clothes are not fash-
ionable, parents are divorced, like poetry instead of football—the list goes on
and on and on. What I have learned from this list is that everyone fits into at
least one of these categories. Therefore we are all different. So, if everyone
is different, there has to be another reason why targets get picked on. I think

it's because some students are getting pleasure out of being mean. If you want to cause pain for someone, you will always be able to find something about them to ridicule. The issue is not who is different, but why does someone think its cool to be cruel.

"If you are getting pleasure out of causing pain, you have some work you need to do and we need to help you.

"I would like to know what you have learned about how to stop bullying? What can you do?" (Write answers on board.) (One of the first responses will be *ignore.*) "How many of you have ever ignored a bully and it worked? How many of you have ever ignored a bully and it didn't work? What works on one bully may not work on the next so you have to have a lot of options." (Write down all answers as quickly as possible.) (If someone says *fight back* you have to stop and deal with that response.) "I have heard from some students that fighting back was the only strategy that worked, but I have to share my concern with you. This is a true story that was told to me by the deputy attorney general of Delaware, Rhonda Denny.

"There was a target who had been abused relentlessly by a bully. The bullying was physical and verbal and it got progressively worse. The target stuffed his anger for months and months and finally one day he couldn't take it any more and he punched the bully in the face. The bully fell back against a concrete pillar and was knocked unconscious. He was rushed to the hospital and fell into a coma. For a while they were not sure that he was going to live. He did survive, but if he hadn't, the target who punched him could have been charged with manslaughter and ended up in a prison setting for years. The risks of fighting are too serious and I am hoping that you will find another way to handle the pain.

"I want to talk to you about the difference between the way girls and boys bully. I have heard that there are five major differences and I would like some feedback from you. When I mention each difference, please nod your heads up and down if you agree, and sideways if you disagree.

"The first difference I've heard is that boys are more physical and sexual and girls are more verbal and emotional and probably more into cyber bullying. (Look for head nods. If there is a lot of disagreement, ask for comments.)

"The second difference I've heard is that boys are more direct and in your face and girls are more indirect and behind your back." (Look for head nods.)

"The third difference I've heard is that if a couple of boys get into a conflict, five minutes later they will go skateboarding together. When girls get into a conflict, it goes on and on and on." (Look for head nods.)

ı difference I've heard is that when boys pick on each other, it's
..., one on one but when girls bully, they get a clique or a whole group
to hurt someone."

(Look for head nods.)

"The fifth difference I've heard is that when boys bully, they pick on
someone outside of their circle of friends. When girls bully, they turn on their
closest friends." (Look for head nods.)

"Ladies, young women, why are we so hard on each other? This meanness
has to stop. Life is tough enough as it is. We are not on this earth to tear each
other down. That is not the purpose of our lives. Please stop the pain!"

"I'm going to teach you a word. Some of you may know it, but it has been
my experience that very few students can give a good definition of the word
empathy.

"Empathy is the capacity to put yourself in somebody else's situation and
imagine how it would be to walk in their shoes. If you broke your leg and had
to walk on crutches and you see someone walking with crutches, you know
what they're going through. But if your friend's parents are getting a divorce
and your parents are not getting a divorce, you can still imagine how painful,
how stressful that is for your friend. That is empathy!

"Empathy is so important that I am going to ask you to practice it, right
now. Please close your eyes. I want you to think about someone you know
who is a target and I want you to put yourself in his or her place. Concentrate on what it would feel like to be that person." (Allow 12–15 seconds to
pass.)

"I'm impressed with the way you focused. Now, I am going to ask the last
question and the first person that raises his/her hand to answer this question
must have a lot of courage, so wait until you hear the question before you
raise your hand. Because of everything we have talked about together this
morning and all the feelings that are going through your mind, is there someone in this room that would like to do some healing? Is there someone in this
room who would be willing to apologize and make amends for something that
you have done or said?"

(Most often several hands will go up. If no hands go up, wait a few seconds
and allow silence to work its pressure. If no hands go up at that point, try
another approach.) "What usually happens at this point is that one person will
serve as a role model and as soon as they share an apology, a lot of hands will
go up and we won't have time to hear them."

(When John or Mary raises their hand, go to that student and stand by
them.)

"Who is the person you wish to apologize to?" (Student will say: "I want
to apologize to Ben." (Ask where Ben is and go to him). "Ben, John has

apologized to you. Do you accept his apology?" (Student will accept the apology.) "Thank you, John and thank you, Ben. You have given us a valuable lesson in remorse and forgiveness. Thank you very, very much. There is a world of difference between 'I apologize' and 'I'm sorry.' Many people say 'I'm sorry' and then they do the same thing, and then they say 'I'm sorry' and they do it again. An apology is a commitment to change your behavior. John is not going to cause pain for Ben anymore. (Call on any others who have raised their hands and repeat the process of honoring and thanking.) (If someone will not accept the apology, ask the person who apologized if they can understand why the apology has not been accepted. Then return to the person who received the apology and ask how long it would take for them to believe that a new behavior is genuine. Take that figure back to the person who apologized and negotiate a time frame for trust to be established.)

"I'm so sorry that we have run out of time for individual apologies. The rest of you will have to apologize in private, but it will still be very meaningful. Would everyone in this room who made an apology, please stand up? It took a lot of courage to admit you had been hurtful and to make amends. Thank you very much.

"Would everyone in this room who owes someone an apology, please stand up?" (Many will stand.) "Please make sure that you apologize to the person who deserves it. Would everyone in this room who feels that they deserve an apology, please stand up? (Some will stand.) "Look around the room and if you are someone who has caused pain for people who are standing, make amends. It will make you feel a lot better, and it will help someone else to heal. When you stop the pain, you are doing your part to change the world.

"Now I have a request for everyone in this class. If you notice that some students in this class are being kinder, that they are changing their behavior, please compliment them in your own creative way. It is not easy to change habits, so if someone is making an effort, honor their good work by letting them know you are a witness.

"I would like to tell you one more story. I read about a boy in California who developed cancer, had chemotherapy, and all of his hair fell out. He decided to drop out of school because he didn't want to be picked on. When his classmates heard about this, 13 boys went to the barbershop and had their heads shaved so this young man could come to school without dread. Whenever I think about those 13 boys, it makes me very proud to be a human being. That is the capacity that we have to care about each other.

"Thank you so much for all that you have taught me. I'm deeply grateful."

End of Session

I want to share one example of the thousands of apologies I have witnessed. At a middle school, a sixth grade boy, Howard, raised his hand and apologized to the entire class. He said, "I know I get really angry sometimes and I say terrible things. I have ADHD and it's not my fault that I'm different. I get very upset when you make fun of me. Everything is so much harder for me because of my problems. No one in this room would want to change places with me. I wish you would just leave me alone."

He reduced everyone to tears with his honesty and courage—students, teachers, counselors, administrators, and me. I checked back with the counselor and learned that students did stop, or at least greatly reduced, bullying toward Howard. He was extremely happy. He now attends an alternative school where his disabilities can be better met.

TIPS ON THE STUDENT EMPOWERMENT SESSION

The biggest challenge you will have is time! You won't be able to get everything in, especially if you have an enthusiastic class and lots of students who wish to participate. You need to allow ten minutes, at the least, to do the empathy/apology section. Every single minute is precious. Explain to the person in charge that you need for the session to start on time. It takes practice to own this content and make decisions on the spot with each unique group of students. You will get better with each session.

My best and worst experiences have happened in middle schools. I can usually tell from the responses to the first question whether the class is going to be a challenge. In some situations, I decide not to present the empathy/close your eyes/apology piece.

Instead, I will read two or three "Letters from Children" that are in Chapter Thirteen of my book "Bullies, Targets & Witnesses." There are 19 such letters that have a stickiness factor.

When participants observe me conducting a session on the first morning of the Training Institute, they can't believe they will be able to make this work when they are facilitators on the third morning. They discover that not only does it work for them but their partners have a successful experience as well. Cherish the privilege of being in the presence of young people who deserve a "cleansing experience."

What is most important about a SES is to engage the students in a dialogue. They have received lectures and speeches. Your gift is to empower them to contribute the information.

A&E produced a Bill Kurtis investigative report entitled "Bullied to Death" in 2000. I was featured in that report and you can see a small segment of my work with students, which can be ordered from Amazon.com. A full length, one hour training DVD of me conducting a Student Empowerment Session can be ordered through my Web site, www.bullysafeusa.com.

I would love to hear from you. Please send me emails and notes about your sessions. suellenfried@hotmail.com. SuEllen Fried, P.O. Box 8527, Prairie Village, KS 66208.

EVALUATION HIGHLIGHTS

BullySafeUSA is a comprehensive school-based bullying intervention program designed to reduce bullying and promote pro-social behavior. The BullySafeUSA program includes a Student Empowerment Session and follow-up activities with students in grades K–12. Students will learn the five kinds of bullying—physical, verbal, emotional, sexual, and cyber bullying. They will learn about the roles of the target, the bully, and the witness and how those roles interchange. An emphasis on actions that witnesses can take is a key component. A new saying, "Sticks and Stones can break your bones, but words can break your heart," is introduced. Students will learn strategies for dealing with bullies, the difference between tattling and reporting, differences between the ways girls and boys bully, and a strong segment on empathy. They will understand bullying is a form of child abuse, peer-to-peer abuse. A goal of the program is to change the culture of the school by reducing the pain, rage, revenge cycle that is connected to bullying. Staff training and parent seminars are offered to support the student empowerment session. An activities guide, "30 Activities for Getting Better at Getting Along," will reinforce the anticipated attitude and behavior changes. To evaluate the effectiveness of the BullySafeUSA program, a program evaluation was conducted in the southeastern United States. Data were collected from approximately 200 students participating in the BullySafeUSA program and approximately 200 students from nearby schools who were not participating in any systematic bullying intervention.

Students in both the treatment and comparison groups completed surveys at the beginning and end of the school year. Shortly after the initial assessment, students in the treatment group began participating in the BullySafeUSA program.

BULLYSAFEUSA

Executive Summary of Positive Program Evaluation Findings

- Students participating in the BullySafeUSA program learned the material presented in the program. They doubled their factual knowledge about bullying after participating in the program for a few months, and after continued participation, on average they were able to correctly respond to 80% of questions about bullying.

- Students participating in the BullySafeUSA program felt an increased sense of responsibility to help the targets of bullying. While approximately half of students indicated that a witness should always help a target before the intervention, over 75% of students indicated that they should always help the targets of bullying after participating in the BullySafeUSA Program. Students who were not participating in any bullying prevention program evidenced no change in their sense of responsibility to help the targets.

- Over the course of the school year, students participating in the BullySafeUSA program continued to feel that there were things they could do to resolve the conflict when the targets of bullies. Students who did not participate in the program felt less control as the school year progressed.

- Over the course of the school year, students participating in the BullySafeUSA program continued to report incidents of bullying to teachers. Students who were participating in the BullySafeUSA program reported incidents of bullying less and less as the school year progressed. By the end of the school year, on average they were almost never reporting bullying.

- Relative to students who were not participating in a prevention program, the students participating in the BullySafeUSA intervention evidenced significant reduction in peer victimization. Peer victimization experiences decreased by 23% in students participating in the BullySafeUSA program. Reductions were apparent in both social and physical victimization.

- Whereas students participating in the BullySafeUSA program evidenced a 15% reduction in bullying behaviors, students not participating in any bullying prevention program evidenced 26% increase in these bullying behaviors over the same time period.

Evaluation Coordinated by Andrew Terranova, Ph.D., Assistant Professor, Department of Psychology, Stephen F. Austin State University, Box 13046 – SFA Station, Nacogdoches, TX 75962, E-Mail: terranova@ sfasu.edu, Telephone: (936) 468-1483.

Chapter 10

Ten Burning Questions
Posed by Educators

In the Fall of 2008, Fried gave several bullying workshops at a conference for the California Association of Private Schools Organization (CAPSO). She asked the participants to jot down on a slip of paper one "burning question" they would like her to address. To her complete amazement, every single attendee wanted to know how to deal with parents who won't believe their child is a bully. Consequently, this will be our first question. The other questions have surfaced, with great frequency, as we have polled educators across the country.

#1 "HOW DO YOU HANDLE THE PARENTS OF A CHILD WHO WON'T ACCEPT THAT THEIR CHILD IS A BULLY?"

As may be expected, many parents of children who engage in all forms of bullying behavior are bullies themselves. They serve as role models for their children's actions and may even encourage their children to be aggressive. The children may hear: "Don't you ever let anyone take advantage of you or put you down." These parents may be the third or fourth generation of people who grew up in an aggressive environment or they may have had painful experiences as targets when they were young and are determined to spare their children that pain. Regardless of the history, we recommend the following options.

The first is a one-on-one session with the parent(s). Do not use the term *bully* or *bullying* in your communication! Begin the conversation by discussing the positive behaviors or skills that you have observed in their child. Then announce that you and the parent want this year to be the most successful possible for their child. You will be partners to make that happen and it is essential to share important information with each other. The parent will know some things about the student that you don't know and you might know some things about their child that they don't know since you see their child in a different setting. Ask the parent to give you information that would be helpful for you to know. Listen attentively and affirm their report. Then bring up some specific behaviors that have come to your attention. Be *very* specific without using the term *bullying*.

Emphasize that it is your responsibility to keep every student in your class safe. Report how you have handled the situations and express your concern if the behavior is continuing. Talk about the school code of conduct and how you are expected to deal with infractions. Ask the parent for their input before you proceed to the next level of consequence. Remind the parent that you are partners and you both want a positive resolution. Come up with a mutually agreed upon action plan that both you and the parent support and suggest that you talk again in a few weeks to keep current on any progress.

Do all that you can to keep the parent as an ally to make this a successful year. If the parent becomes belligerent, suggest that you both think about the conversation, what you have heard from each other and agree to have another meeting at a future date. On that occasion, ask the school counselor or an administrator to be present to support your perspective and concern for other children. Explain the steps that will be taken to avoid suspension or expulsion. You might recommend an appointment with a physician or a therapist or some testing. Maintain how important it is to deal with issues before they become more severe.

You might gain some support from a parent by asking if behaviors of concern would be acceptable in the workplace. If childhood is a training ground for adulthood, it becomes easier to see what is acceptable and what isn't.

The second option that we recommend is a meeting with all of the parents. Parents of bullies have been characterized as authoritarian, cold, unresponsive, distant, domineering, demanding, directive, or verbally and/ or physically and/or sexually abusive, doling out severe punishment for perceived misbehavior. These parents are very likely to bring the same personality traits to the classroom when meeting with teachers. For these parents we propose a different approach. We suggest that the classroom teacher call a meeting of all the parents in the class and that at least one parent or caregiver be required to attend. Either a school administrator or counselor should also be in attendance.

For a suggested outline, see Appendix C.

If the parents of the bullies do not attend the class meeting ask for the cooperation of the school administration to have a personal meeting with the parents to report to them what was discussed at the class meeting.

#2 "WHAT SHOULD I DO ABOUT A COLLEAGUE WHO IS A BULLY?"

Developing a professional code of ethics with the faculty is an effective way of establishing accountability.

Educators have observed that teachers who bully are usually new teachers reacting to overwhelming frustrations or tenured teachers who are very set in their ways. It is the responsibility of the principal to deal with a teacher who bullies students. There are principals who know of staff members who engage in bullying but because of tenure cannot dismiss them. Many principals have shared their frustrations and their efforts to move these teachers into office positions where they will not be with students in the classroom.

Joel Klein, the chancellor of the New York City Public School system has taken radical, expensive measures to remove tenured teachers who should not be in the classroom for good reasons, including bullying behavior. They continue to receive their salaries but do not interact with students in classrooms.

Other principals, who do not have the power to terminate inappropriate teachers, are eager to find a solution. We have several suggestions to offer.

For the new teacher, assign an experienced teacher to be a collegial coach. This new teacher can confide in the coach for mentoring without fear of reprisal. Teachers who have learned the ropes of classroom management can share effective techniques for maintaining order and preventing stressful issues from arising. The following Web site offers extensive resources on the topic: www.northern.edu/ois/Mentor.htm.

For issues with the tenured teacher, schedule a staff training on the subject of bullying prevention and insist that the trainer cover this specific topic. It is best to have an outside trainer who can make generic recommendations without knowing the particular teachers. The core of the training is to focus on changing the culture—by changing attitudes, feelings, and behaviors. While children are the focus of these changes, every adult must model these changes. We cannot have expectations for students that adults are not prepared to honor for themselves.

At this training, recommend that when any staff member, including nonteaching staff, *witnesses* a teacher bullying a student, they are to report that documented information to the principal. If we are asking student witnesses to take risks, staff members must be willing to do the same. The principal can use the collection of documented reports to contact the teacher.

An unexpected solution came when Mary Fischer, a BullySafeUSA colleague, was conducting a student empowerment session. Toward the end, a teacher who had been listening intently to the definitions and descriptions of bullying, spontaneously apologized to her students for her bullying behavior. The forgiving students were so touched by her repentance that they rushed to give her hugs, and a tearful conclusion was had by all. Mary reports that the atmosphere of the classroom completely changed, and the teacher, her students, and their parents enjoyed a splendid year.

A final recommendation is that the following email that Fried received from a student be copied and placed in every teacher's mail box. It is reprinted without grammar, punctuation or spelling corrections.

I wanted some information regarding a teacher who is the bully in her classroom to students as young as I. I am depressed and get sweats right before I go into her classroom. My mother and the principal is aware of this teachers lacks but the teacher still abuses us in her class, the principle said that it is very hard to get rid of a teacher even if they know that this teacher is not fit to teach, this teacher has files of complaints from kids and parents but nothing is been looked on. Am I the only kid in the world that has a teacher who bullies? Are my classmates now, before me and after me will have no choice to just deal with the abusive ways, because it is just too much work or details to go through just to discipline a teacher, it is just not fair. This teacher has been teaching more than 25 years as my mom had her once and it was an unpleasant experience for her too and I am experiencing it. I just feel very strongly that this is so unfair, that teachers can do to us and say things that hurt our feelings and that is okay, if we the student did any of that disrespect to the teacher we encounter almost an world war III from the principle, teachers, and parents while this teacher do to us and just laughs. I don't want nothing to do with science anymore, I also don't respect teachers as much as I did, I always respected them like a second parent but this teacher changed almost all my thinking of my mind. Can you help me? Do you have any materials I can share with my classmates and may be help the principle to do something about our problem? This is a pro-bully for she have been doing it for almost 30 years. 20, 30 thousands had to endure her and more, I pray for my teacher to STOP. She makes us cry every time.

#3 "HOW DO I HANDLE A GROUP OF GIRL BULLIES WHO ARE A REAL CHALLENGE?"

A spate of books, such as *Queen Bees and Wannabees* and *Odd Girl Out* and movies such as *Mean Girls* have added a whole new dimension to our understanding of the term *relational aggression,* or RA, as it is widely called. It is a type of psychological abuse in which harm is caused through or to relationships. Carol Gilligan argues that boys are socialized to value achievement as their most important goal while girls are socialized to value affiliation as their most important goal.

Because it is related to increased depression, lower academic performance, increased suicidal ideation, and increased anger and sadness it must be confronted. Friendships, relationships, and affiliations dominate female behavior. Beginning in preschool, little girls use "I won't be your friend" as their strongest leverage to get what they want. As they grow older, they become more covert, but the threat is the same.

We believe in confronting girls about their cruelty by discussing the five differences between the way girls and boys bully as described by Fried in Chapter Nine. Preferably, at the beginning of the year—or sadly, when a crisis occurs—a teacher, perhaps with a counselor, could invite all the girls in the class to have a picnic lunch in the room. Try to arrange with the physical education teacher to keep the boys for at least a forty-five minute to an hour period. Push the chairs out of the way, spread several blankets on the floor and create an intimate space.

Start the session with some kind of an "ice-breaker" that rearranges their typical groupings. One example is to ask all of the girls who are the oldest in their family to sit together, the middle children to sit together, the youngest children to sit together, and the only children to sit together. Direct them to share with each other what's good and not-so-good about their birth order.

After a few minutes bring all the girls together in a circle and begin a new conversation by asking girls to mention women in their lives that they admire. Pick up on the caring, nurturing, generous qualities that are mentioned and talk about what gifts loving women bring to the world.

Then bring up the "five differences" between the way girls and boys bully and ask if there is any truth to the statements. Ask if any of them have sisters or close friends who have known what that feels like. Gently lead them into a more personal conversation about hurtfulness they have witnessed or experienced. Ask them what they can do to stop the pain.

When girls can recognize how much they resort to sabotage and backstabbing to cause pain, how capricious they are in the way they banish a long-standing friendship, admit that a slight can grow into a schism and last for years without resolution, and acknowledge that a clique can supply the courage to do and say things you never would do on your own, they can begin to examine their behavior and make change.

The Ophelia Project and Girl Scouts USA have developed wonderful materials and programs. Bringing the mothers and daughters together to experience a reading group with each other can serve a multitude of purposes. Choose a book appropriate for the ages of the girls.

#4 "HOW CAN I HELP A STUDENT UNDERSTAND THAT SHE/HE IS BULLYING OTHERS?"

Perhaps the question should be reframed. The real question is "How can I help a student to choose more successful behavior?" If all behavior serves a purpose, what is the student gaining by being hurtful to others? The solution is not to coerce the student to admit that they are "bad" or that they are a "bully" but to discover their intention.

Arrange to spend some private time with the student and approach the conversation with the visualization of the student with a "hook in his/her mouth." Are they acting out because they are trying to avoid pain of some kind? Are they acting out because they are getting some reward for their behavior? Are they under a lot of stress and taking it out on other people? Are they acting out because they lack empathy or a moral code? The student is probably expecting you to make some judgment about them. Instead you are trying to understand what they need and how you can help them meet that need. Ask questions to get at the motivation.

If you can reach a point where the student believes you are coming from concern for him/her as well as for others, you can focus on the unacceptable behaviors. Always refer to the specific behaviors and never use the term bully or bullying. Ask the student if s/he feels like they have ever crossed the line. Be sure to bring empathy into the discussion. Express belief that the student has the power to control inappropriate behavior. Sometimes students run out of impulse control at the end of the day. Create a special hand signal that you can use with each other for times of stress and times of praise. When s/he is getting stressed and about to lose control, have s/he give you a hand signal. Ask the student to take a message to the office. Make a prior contact with the secretary so she understands s/he is coming to the office for stress relief. When you notice that s/he is exerting self-control, give a special hand signal to let the student know you are aware.

#5 "HOW CAN I GET STUDENTS TO REPORT WHEN THEY ARE BEING BULLIED OR WHEN THEY WITNESS OTHERS BEING BULLIED?"

We have addressed this in different sections of our book but we will pull together several recommendations that we have made. First and foremost have a class meeting on the subject of bullying. A Student Empowerment Session has made a dramatic difference for thousands of students.

Issues of confidentiality must be discussed, and the person reported to has to earn credibility with the students. Assure all of the students that a reporter of abusive behavior will not be put in jeopardy by divulging their report to the offender. Remind students of how many tragedies have been averted when reports have been made to adults.

Have a discussion about the difference between *tattling* and *reporting*. Remind the students that tattling is when you are trying to get someone IN trouble and reporting is when you are trying to get someone OUT of trouble. At the elementary school level, it might take repeating the question many times before it becomes the new social norm. With older children, train them to work with younger children on this issue. By working on this topic with younger students they will come to a better understanding of how important it is to reach out to adults. Also, stress the consequences for our society when criminals are protected by people who won't "snitch." Explain that logically, the more students who report, the less likely it will be for the offender to know who was the source.

Assure targets that it is not a weakness to involve adults. Students who bully have problems and they make problems for targets that require adult intervention. It is far worse to suffer regularly, to lose confidence and self-esteem, to dread coming to school, and to become depressed or filled with rage. Schools are obligated to provide a safe environment for all students and that includes bullying.

You might also want to do the witness training exercise from Chapter Nine if your class has not participated in a Student Empowerment Session.

At all costs, never dismiss a report that may have required a great deal of courage to be given to you. Honor it with trust and respect.

#6 WHAT CAN I DO ABOUT CYBER BULLYING THAT IS NOT OCCURRING AT SCHOOL?

Parry Afteb, an Internet lawyer, is the executive director of WiredSafety, a valuable resource on this topic. WiredSafety.org informs us that 90 percent of middle school students have had their feelings hurt online, 75 percent have visited a Web site bashing another student, and 40 percent have had their password(s) stolen and changed by a bully. Students have their own cyberspace shorthand language, a language that few parents and adults understand.

Cyber bullying has raised serious issues for law enforcement, school officials, child protection, parental supervision, and freedom of speech advocates. These issues are being addressed in a variety of ways in different situations and locations. A social dilemma exists that has not been resolved. Many school administrators believe that the school cannot and should not be held responsible for every message that every student sends from their home computer. That is a daunting responsibility for our schools to assume.

On the other hand, many students who are being victimized by cyber bullying are reluctant to share that information with their parents in fear that the computer will be taken off limits for them. Most parents are not savvy about the various ways that electronic technology can be used to inflict trauma and don't know how to monitor their children's usage, even if they wanted to. Schools may be the only recourse for some students where consequences can come into play.

Students are reporting many different ways in which access to the Internet has produced appalling acts of cruelty. For example, "A student found a way to gain my password and proceeded to send a series of hateful letters to my classmates without my knowing about it. I had no idea why people were so ugly to me. My friends wouldn't speak to me and other kids would curse me out."

In another incident, a boy posted a horrific essay about a girl on a Web site that invited visitors to express hatred about her. Word spread quickly and soon it was the talk of the school. Although the posting had not occurred at school, a school administrator checked out the site after a number of students brought it to his attention. The essay was so cruel and damaging that school officials felt some responsibility to intervene. They met with the girl involved, and then the boy, and both sets of parents.

The boy felt deep remorse when he realized that what had seemed like an impulsive and insignificant act had had such a profound effect on the girl. He contacted the Web site manager and asked to have the essay removed, but the Web site manager refused, saying that to do so would be a violation of free speech and would constitute censorship.

The very least that schools can do is to hold parent seminars on the topic of cyber bullying. The PTA, PTO, or the school district can bring in experts with the most current knowledge who can answer troubling questions from parents. Schools can make it clear that if they receive evidence of cyber bullying that is abusive to a student, they will take the harshest measures possible.

The school can also engage students in the solution. Involve them in a discussion about what they have read on the topic, what their greatest fears are, and how they can repair harm that has taken place. A student task force could organize a student bill of rights regarding cyber bullying. If students would make a commitment not to pass on stinging, cowardly, devastating comments on the Internet, a lot of pain could be prevented. Students should also be informed that technology is becoming more sophisticated every day and anonymous bullying can be detected and exposed.

Involve students in a discussion about what they have read on the topic and what their greatest fears are, creating a cyber code of conduct they would sign, and a discussion of how they can repair harm that has taken place.

States from Rhode Island to Oregon are grappling with cyber bullying language and how much responsibility to place on schools. "The kids are forcing our hands to do something legislatively," said Rhode Island State Sen. John Tassoni. However, Steven Brown, executive director of the Rhode Island branch of the American Civil Liberties Union, said it will be difficult to draft a cyber bullying law that doesn't infringe on free speech rights.

South Carolina, however, passed a law that requires school districts to define bullying and outline policies and repercussions for the behavior, including cyber bullying. One school district has proposed punishments from warnings to expulsion. The father of a son who committed suicide because of cyber bullying is advocating for laws that would allow victims and their families to pursue civil penalties. This issue will continue to plague us. Will we be able to convince young people to manage their behavior or will we have to take draconian measures, as officials in some states are doing with sexting, to curb senseless, cruel cyber bullying.

#7 WHAT IF MY PRINCIPAL DOESN'T SUPPORT ME WHEN I AM TRYING TO DEAL WITH BULLYING SITUATIONS?

Invite the principal to attend a Student Empowerment Session or to sit in on a brief class discussion that you lead about bullying. Be sure to cover the five types of bullying. Come up with some questions for the students that you think will produce the most persuasive argument for your concerns.

Most school counselors are very attuned to bullying problems. Enlist your counselor to work with you on a convincing strategy. Knowing what will grab your principal's interest is key. Will it be parent anger, the threat of a lawsuit, or the competitive challenge of another school in the district that is making great strides in bullying prevention?

Research the particular angle that will have the most impact on your principal's decision. There is an enormous amount of information available if you are willing to take the time to find it.

Give your students a writing assignment about bullying Have them give examples of bullying they have experienced or witnessed. Have them include bullying incidents on the bus, the playground, the cafeteria, the bathroom, and other hot spots. Ask them to give some suggestions on how the school should handle bullying problems. To protect their privacy, have them make create a pseudonym (like Mark Twain for Samuel Clemens). Share the essays with the principal.

Explain to the principal how you intend to design a bullying prevention plan for your classroom, based on the information you have collected from your students and their parents. List some very specific support you believe would be helpful to your vision, maybe just one item to begin with. Keep the principal informed of the progress you are making with your plan, especially if there are fewer disruptions, fewer referrals to the principal, and test scores are improving. Use data to show the correlation between improved social behavior and academic achievement.

Be prepared to handle as much discipline within the classroom as possible. Speak with the vice principal, if your school has one, to see if you can find a sympathetic advocate in that position. If you happen to have an acquaintance with the president of the PTA or PTO, sound that person out to see if s/he is concerned about bullying. Try to build a network. Don't forget the power of The Law of the Few.

#8 WHY AREN'T PUNISHMENTS FOR BULLIES HARSHER? WHY ARE THE TARGETS THE ONES WHO HAVE TO CHANGE SCHOOLS?

It is very unjust that many families whose children are being bullied bear the greatest burden, by moving or transferring their child away from the abusive school situation. Sometimes they turn to home schooling.

A recent study released by the U.S. Department of Education estimates that as of 2007, 1.5 million children or 2.9 percent of all school-age children are being educated at home, up from 850,000 in 1999. *USA TODAY* released the data in an article in May 2009. A significant shift occurred in the ratio of girls being home schooled. In 1999, it was 49 percent boys, 51 percent girls. Currently girls represent 58 percent compared to 42 percent of boys. There is speculation that mean-girl bullying is an underlying reason. In fact, 21 percent of parents cited concerns about the school environment, whereas 17 percent cited dissatisfaction with academic instruction. To provide religious or moral instruction was identified by 36 percent of parents.

Parents who are willing to challenge the school hierarchy and succeed in their demands must be persistent and realize that it will take a great deal of patience and fortitude. When all else fails, some parents have taken the legal route and been victorious, but it can be extremely expensive and very time consuming. It appears that more cases have been decided in favor of the school systems than families.

As for harsher penalties for bullies, again and again we come back to prevention and intervention at the earliest possible stage of a child's development. When do we give up on a youngster who never had a caring adult who believed in his/her worth?

Data gathered in the National Pre-kindergarten Study (NPS) presents expulsion data from all 40 states that fund prekindergarten programs. In classrooms where teachers had no access to psychologists or psychiatrists, 10.8 prekindergarteners per 1,000 were expelled. If we are expelling prekindergarteners, what is this saying about our ability to manage unruly children? And what kinds of interventions were used before expulsion?

What kind of discipline is most effective? Our harshest punishment is expulsion, but how can we congratulate ourselves when we remove an incorrigible bully from our school and throw him/her into our neighborhood, our community, with no supervision, to inflict even greater harm on more people.

Alternative schools can be an answer for many young people. Extremely aggressive children must be held accountable and placed in a setting that can deal with their issues. The targets stay in their familiar surroundings and the young perpetrators are given a second chance. There are exemplary models of alternative schools, which have turned many young people's lives around. In smaller communities where alternative schools are not available, regional residential treatment facilities might serve their needs. The next step, unfortunately, is prison. One out of every 99 persons in the United States is in prison. What happened, or didn't happen, to those inmates when they were in school?

Even the juvenile justice system is moving toward rehabilitation in small groups, constant therapeutic interventions, and minimal force. Coercive punishment is giving way to a lighter hand with positive results. The Missouri Model is a prime example of such a promising reform movement that is being emulated by other states. When someone becomes unruly, the other youths are trained to talk him down. Tim Decker, director of the Division of Youth Services in Missouri, has pioneered this award winning approach. His recognized efforts are even being applied successfully in adult prisons. If these methods are working with young men and women who have become part of the criminal population, why can't we use them with students who haven't reached that stage?

#9 "HOW DO I HANDLE A BULLY WHOSE FATHER IS THE PRINCIPAL OR SUPERINTENDENT OR A MEMBER OF THE SCHOOL BOARD?"

Chances are the child has been given a free ride for much too long because of the parent's status. The child has paid a serious price for the deferential treatment. From the moment that son or daughter enters your classroom, s/he must be treated exactly the same as all other students and expectations for appropriate behavior never lowered. That will be in the best interest of the student, the best interest of the classmates, and in the long run, the best interest of the parent.

Request a parent conference with the principal and guide the conversation the same as in dealing with a parent in question #1. You might be the one person who is capable of administering the "tough love," the firm hand the child desperately needs. If the principal challenges you, respond by saying you assumed that you would be expected to honor the school code of conduct for all students, as you have always done. Document every entanglement you have with the student and the principal in detail. Contact the president of the teacher's union when trouble first starts brewing and alert that person to a possible problem. Hold to your standards and work diligently not to become adversarial with the principal. This is where past performance will serve you well.

#10 "WHAT IS THE BEST WAY FOR ME TO APPROACH THE CLASSROOM ABOUT BULLYING?"

The best way is to bring it up at the beginning of the year, before bullying occurs. Once situations have erupted, and children have become identified as bullies and/or targets, the discussion won't seem as generic. Speak openly and honestly about expectations.

Remember Mrs. Gardner, who at the very beginning of the semester, told her students that her highest priority was for students to treat each other with respect and dignity. "We need this room to feel completely safe so you can learn as much as possible." Talk about the classroom being a bully-free zone!

Bring in an outside speaker who will reinforce your approach. Find ways to connect bullying issues to various subject matter, English, math, social studies, etc. Involve the students. English can easily be connected to literature, books, and stories about bullying.

Social studies can include the frequent newspaper articles that appear about bullying, or even better, about people who make a difference in other people's lives.

Math could be an opportunity to use the social norm approach and survey the class about their perceptions of student attitudes about bullying. Check out the National Center for Social Norming for survey questions. Have them estimate what percentage believe students treat each other respectfully, what percentage believe that students have the right to feel safe, and what percentage believe that students will support classmates who are being bullied. After the surveys have been turned in, have the class compile the perceptions and compare them with the class averages.

Above all, model the behavior you want your students to exhibit and affirm individual and classroom exemplary behavior. Be the thermostat to set the tone.

Chapter 11

Parents as Protectors, Partners, and Change Agents

The hardest part of being a parent is when your child is being bullied at school.

—Martin, a parent

PARENTS AS PROTECTORS

Parent of a Target

How will you know if your child is being bullied? If your child continually finds excuses not to go to school, that is a major clue. If your child's behavior changes dramatically, by becoming aggressive or withdrawn, that is another indication.

The best, of course, will be if your child confides in you. Many children will not report to their parents that they are being bullied. They are reluctant to confess that they have become a target because they think they should be able to take care of bullying problems themselves. They don't want to risk losing your approval. Other children are concerned that their parents will get too upset and do something to make the situation worse. Lastly, they fear that you will dismiss what they have to say and do nothing to protect them.

If you are fortunate enough that your child reports to you they are being bullied, accept that report as a gift. Children trust you to be a protector. Do not tell them to ignore the bully. All children who have ever been bullied tried to ignore it before they came to you. They deserve a more sophisticated response. Let your child know that bullying is serious and you will be there to support them until the bullying stops.

Physical and Verbal Bullying

Plan A should be to empower your children to resolve the situation themselves. Begin by asking questions and document everything you learn. Write down names, dates, places, and the types of bullying they describe, which you might need in the future.

Questions should include "When and where does the bullying occur most often"? "What is the form of bullying—physical, verbal, emotional, gender, cyber?" "What student or students are involved?" "Are there any other students present?" "Are there any adults who are aware of what is happening to you?" "Is there more than one bully?" "How have you responded?" "Has it ever worked?" "Does the student(s) who is bullying you, pick on others as well?" "How do other students deal with the bully?" "Have you ever seen someone else handle the bully successfully?" "What did they do or say?" "Have you had an idea that you haven't tried yet?" "What if we role play?" "You be the bully and I'll be you."

Role-playing has helped many students by having a script they could practice with their parents. It's difficult to come up with zingers when you're in the throes of pain, but if you can rehearse some lines in advance, it's easier to deflect the situation in the moment.

We talk to students about the difference between a passive response, an aggressive response, and an assertive response. For instance, if someone says: "Your hair is so ugly," a passive response would be to internalize the put-down and be ashamed of your hair. An aggressive response would be to retort with: "Well, my hair may be ugly, but it's not nearly as ugly as your face." Now, *you* have become the bully!

There are numerous possibilities for an assertive response. "When I looked in the mirror this morning, I had the very same thought—I am having a really bad hair day," or "You have such terrific hair. You are so lucky, I sure wish I had hair like you!" or "Thank you for noticing my hair problem, do you have a suggestion for a stylist (or barber)?" or "How would you feel if someone said that to you?" or "What's going on with you that you have a need to do this?" Many students have learned to say "So" or "Thank you" or "Have a good day."

There is a marvelous little book by Alice Cohen-Posey, *How to Handle Bullies, Teasers and Other Meanies,* that gives excellent suggestions for come-backs and one-liners. Get a copy and use it to find a phrase that feels comfortable for your child.

Some children just can't foster the nerve to respond verbally to their tormentor. If that is the case, nonverbal strategies need to be in your child's repertoire. Body language can reveal obvious cues that reward bullies. To make the point we tell children: "When you lower your chin, the bullies win. When you lift your chin, then you can win." One parent helped her son by giving him the imagery of a suit of armor. She suggested that he imagine himself wearing a protective metal shield to deflect all of the verbal barbs. She even went to a costume shop and bought him one to wear around the house to practice feeling invincible—and it worked!

We recommend that you expose your child to the martial arts, such as karate, tae kwon do, or tai chi. We have heard wonderful reports from parents whose children blossomed when they experienced the centering and respect that are part of these eastern forms of movement. Posture is a noticeable feature that signals strength or vulnerability to a bully.

If you can convince your son or daughter that bullies are the one with the problem, not them, you will have made real headway. Ask your child what he/she suspects is the reason why the student is bullying. A child psychiatrist, Dr. Richard Davis, found that parents were amazed at how quickly the bullying problem could be solved when the target child gives up the self-blame that accompanies bullying. When children who have failed to stand up for themselves become confident enough to take control, their problem can be solved directly.

A thoughtful young boy at Scarsdale Middle School shared his personal epiphany. He told us that all through elementary school, where he was a favorite target, he tried to pretend that he wasn't bothered, but his body betrayed his vulnerability. The summer before he attended middle school, something happened that he couldn't explain. "I grew myself up inside." When he started sixth grade, he didn't have to pretend how he felt, because he just didn't care how the bullies behaved. "I decided that I was going to be in charge of who I was, not someone else." The bullying ceased.

Explain to your child how powerful it makes bullies feel if they can incite you to cry. Tears give bullies enormous satisfaction. Tears are a normal response to a painful predicament, but if there is any way your child can postpone the tears until s/he reaches the bathroom at school or his/her bedroom at home, it will deny bullies the sense of power they crave.

Humor has been a magical solution for many students. Nothing takes the steam out of a bully's tirade like a joke. One boy shared his formula for success. He kept making the bully laugh, until his tormentor relinquished his jibes and became his friend instead.

Storytelling is an excellent tool. Children love to hear stories from your youth. Share incidents that occurred when you were their age. Knowing that you once struggled with hurtful peers and now you have become this strong, capable, caring adult is inspiring, to say the least.

Emotional Bullying

The strategies for dealing with the nonverbal manifestations of emotional bullying—such as making faces, pointing, staring, flicking someone off, hand signs, snickering, drawing pictures, and writing notes—are the same as suggested for physical and verbal. But when bullying comes in the form of psychological abuse—such as rejection, isolation, exclusion, and/or ostracizing, new coping skills must come into play.

James Garbarino, in his book, *See Jane Hit,* claims that "Human beings are social creatures and to feel right about themselves they need to be in relationships. This seems to be particularly true of girls, who tend to be more affiliative than boys."

The arc of female gossip and rumor spreading can reach horrific proportions, but the withdrawal of contact can be absolutely devastating. Sometimes girls drift apart as their new interest in boys attracts like-minded friends. The kind of meanness that singles someone out for isolation that is intentional, and often without apparent reason, is in a category of its own. How can a girl respond assertively to a clique of girls who were her friends on Tuesday but will have nothing to do with her on Wednesday? In addition to abandonment, girls will resort to cyber bullying to plot a full-scale orchestration of exclusion. Though girls have finely honed their expertise in this category of rejection, boys are not exempt from isolation from their peer group.

Our advice for parents on this particular form of bullying is complex. You can demand that someone stop hitting your child, but how can you demand that someone accept and include your child as a friend?

Encourage your daughter or son to find a friend or group of friends outside of school. Perhaps a youth group, a dancing class, a chess club, or a community service project will open up new connections. Help your child develop a talent, a passion for an interest, a focus on an idea that's worthy of pursuit. A pet that offers unconditional love can make a tremendous difference. One friend, one trustworthy friend, can be life-changing.

A fascinating Australian study on friendship found that older people with a large circle of friends were 22 percent less likely to die during the study period than those with fewer friends. In the same New York Times article, Harvard researchers reported that strong social ties could promote brain health. Rebecca G. Adams, a professor of sociology at the University of North Carolina, Greensboro, claims that "Friendship has a bigger impact on our psychological well-being than family relationships." These and other studies corroborate the fact that friendship has a profound psychological effect. This information underscores the need for parents to add friendships to their "must do" list for their children.

Above all, tell your child that bullies' motives are most probably unfathomable and dwelling on how to regain their favor will not be fruitful. Moving forward with a strong sense of self and personal resolve will do more to diminish their power than anything else.

Ask your child's permission to talk to the school counselor who may have some ideas to engage your daughter or son in a project with another student in need of a friend. Maybe he or she could tutor a younger student or a special ed youngster who needs some extra attention.

Reassure your child of their virtues, authentic attributes they can accept as true. Do not shower them with pity but rather search with them for a workable result.

Sexual Bullying

Sexual harassment is a form of discrimination prohibited by Title VII of the Civil Rights Act of 1964 and Title IX of the Education Amendments of 1972. Sexual harassment is a term familiar to children but usually empty of definition. The legal definition consists of unwelcome sexual advances, requests for sexual favors, sexually motivated physical conduct, or other verbal or physical conduct or communication.

Be sure to document any infraction with date, place, and time. Your children will be more likely to report any harassment to you if you had previous frank and open sexual conversations with your daughters and your sons. If they sense you are uncomfortable about the subject, they will protect your discomfort.

Cyber Bullying

The National Crime Prevention Council has an excellent Web site with excellent information and recommendations—www.ncpc.org. Some of the recommendations include having an important discussion with your teens about the risks. Keep communication open so they will trust you with any cyber bullying they experience. Advise your teens never to post or share personal information online and to refuse to pass along cyber bullying messages to others.

Monitor your teen's use of the computer by installing it in a central location where you can have access. Learn how to block cyber bullying messages through your Internet service provider, social network site, or chat room moderator. If your teen is being cyber bullied, be sure to save the evidence that you may need for reporting purposes.

In your role as protector, be reminded that Plan A was to empower your child to manage his/her own problem, no matter which form of bullying. In spite of all your efforts, this doesn't always work. Plan B could be contacting the parent of the bully, or the bully, directly. Many experts warn against such action. There are some notable risks that we will spell out.

Before you contact the parent of the bully, keep in mind that some child bullies are the product of a home where bullying is the norm. Such a parent might support their child's behavior, indeed they may have instructed him/her to be tough, not to show any signs of weakness, and to strike first to avoid being on the defensive. That same parent may try to intimidate you and cause you to lose your calm demeanor. S/he may inform his/her child of your call. Either of these responses could make the situation worse.

At parent seminars, when this question of strategy emerges, parents always say they would want to know if their child is bullying. On several occasions, parents have volunteered how embarrassing it was to have the school identify their child as a bully to another child when the parent of the target is a friend of theirs. If you think your friend would prefer to hear about the problem from you, practice your approach and try it out with a spouse or neighbor before you try it out with your friend.

Several creative parents have described how they solved the bullying problem with other parents. One parent invited the family of the bully, including the offender, to a picnic supper. The parents made a pleasant connection and continued socializing with their children in hand. As designed, the family relationship neutralized the tormenting.

A father told of being furious about the abuse his son was experiencing at the hand of an extremely cruel boy. The father marched up to school, demanding that the offender be expelled, only to learn that the bully had recently lost his father in a tragic automobile accident and had been on a rampage against everyone ever since. The father of the target went home and invited the bully to go on a fishing trip the next weekend with him and his son.

A number of mothers and fathers have confronted the bullies of their children directly and forcefully, at school and outside of school successfully. Consider many options, just as your child needs to do.

Plan C involves contacting the school. Assume that the school is your ally and will take responsible action. Start by contacting the teacher. If, for some reason, the teacher is not responsive, call the counselor, then the vice principal, the principal, the superintendent, all the way up the ladder until someone takes responsibility to stop the bullying. No matter how upset you are, get your feelings under control and handle every encounter in a respectful way. Accusations tend to make people defensive. Be appreciative of support. Be sure to keep your documentation current, including the nonresponses of any staff you contact.

If that chain of command doesn't bring results, contact the school board, and as a last resort, consider engaging a lawyer. Your child needs to appreciate that you will not cease to pursue accountability until the bullying stops.

Many parents have given up on their school system and enrolled their child in a different school or chosen to home school their student.

If your child does not report any bullying situations to you, as a protector, you must still be alert for any indication that bullying is taking place. At the beginning of this chapter we listed some informative clues. If you notice any behavior changes or excuses to avoid school, initiate a calm conversation with your child. If information isn't forthcoming, a visit to your child's doctor might be in order. Share your suspicions and concerns in advance of the appointment.

Parent of a Bully

Many parents have been shocked to learn that their child who had never been linked with physical, verbal, emotional, or gender/sexual bullying has found cyber bullying to be very seductive. The technological anonymity unleashes behaviors that had been previously unthinkable. Because most parents have not been exposed to the power of cruelty that students inflict through texting, MySpace, Facebook, cell phones, etc., you may be completely unaware of your child's involvement. It is imperative to have a discussion about this pervasive form of bullying and insist that communication you would not dare to make in person is off limits via technology.

What if your child is a bully? Get your emotions under control. Ask yourself a series of demanding questions—Is your child under a lot of stress? Has he/she joined a new group of friends who act out aggressively? Has some great disappointment or frustration left a residue of unresolved anger? Could your child have been a target and has resorted to bullying as a self-defense technique? Has he/she decided that being aggressive is the only way to survive the schoolyard battlefield? Could your child be imitating behaviors from home? Is bullying a parenting style? Is there any sibling abuse occurring? An inquiring, constructive conversation is in order. Determining the root of the bullying behavior is your goal. Begin by citing the qualities you admire in your child and expressing concern about behavior that is out of character, if this is, in truth, the case. You want your child to believe that you have his/her best interest at heart. This dialogue should not be judgmental but one of information gathering. You will need good communication skills to make this work, and being critical at this point will not be helpful. This is a good time to practice your own empathy skills and put yourself inside your child's being. If our behavior is a response to our thought process, it's imperative to get through to your son or daughter's thought process. Once you discover why they are engaging in bullying behavior, you can devise a thoughtful reaction.

Don't attempt to uncover the problem and solve it in the same conversation. Give yourself some time to digest what you have learned. Getting feedback from another family member could be very valuable. Never be reluctant to reach out for professional assistance if you feel stymied.

Sometimes it's the family culture that needs dissecting. Elizabeth Sweeney found increasing evidence of a family connection with bullying. She reviewed research from England, Germany, Norway, Japan, South Africa, and the United States primarily involving children between the ages of 9 and 16. In her findings, published in August 2008, she reported that "children raised by authoritarian parents—parents who are demanding, directive and unresponsive—are the most prone to act out bullying behavior.

She also wrote, that "children who experience hostility, abuse, physical discipline and other aggressive behaviors by their parents are more likely to model that behavior in their peer relationships. Children learn from their parents how to behave and interact with others. If they're learning about aggression and angry words at home, they will tend to use these behaviors as coping mechanisms when they interact with peers."

On the flip side are the parents of bullies who are caring, loving, and nurturing. They don't understand their children's antisocial behavior and are at their wits end, desperate for help. They are losing control of their children and they are in constant conflict with them at home over a broad range of antisocial behavior, including bullying.

Key findings of a report published by the not-for-profit Parentline Plus in the United Kingdom in 2004 were based on 900 calls to their 24-hour free helpline. "80 percent of the parents talked about high levels of conflict with their child, 69 percent spoke about their child's high level of anger, and 77 percent reported that their child was having a problems at school, with more than half saying that their child had been excluded or was playing truant."

Parents of bullies were three times more likely to report that their child was lying and twice as likely to mention stealing, smoking, and drug abuse. Conflict with peers was another concern, with 20 percent talking about their children being in with a "bad crowd." One typical parent called in reporting that she and her husband were "at the end of their tether" concerning their 15-year-old daughter who was engaged in underage sex, bullying behavior at school, and was verbally abusive at home.

Don Braun, the chief executive of Parentline Plus, said, "These findings concern us greatly. Not only are parents of bullies telling us they are losing control, but the statistics demonstrate the very high levels of conflict both within the families, the school and the community. It is essential that when schools and communities develop policies to cut down on bullying and to ensure community safety, the families of bullies are recognized as needing responsive and appropriate help with their family life, and not further isolation."

Our advice for parents of younger children, or children who still respect your authority, is to be proactive in your relationship with them. Mobilize their feelings of empathy and/or reduce their stress. It will be easier to get in touch with the thought process of a younger child and to set limits and impose boundaries and consequences for unacceptable behaviors. Limit the time your child spends engaged in video games, TV, music, or movies with violent content.

Let your children know that you care about their needs, but you will not allow them to cause pain for someone else. Do not become an enabler.

Here is a checklist for parents to think about. Does your child get pleasure from taunting others; enjoy spreading rumors; seek power and control over others; act out anger by hitting, kicking, or damaging property; play on other's insecurity; use words to humiliate or ridicule others; refuse to admit mistakes and correct them; have serious problems with siblings; witness abusive behavior in your home; lack a sense of humor; lack empathy; or find it pleasurable to torture animals?

If you can be brutally honest and see a pattern of your child's behavior in this check list, you are on a constructive path for change. If you find yourself in a state of constant irritation and frustration, consider professional help.

Speak with personnel at your child's school. Inform them about the steps you have taken and find out how you could work together to bring about a change in attitude. School personnel will respect you for recognizing the situation and will make a special effort to cooperate. The earlier you confront the problem, the sooner it can become resolved.

Parent of a Witness

Most likely, your child has been a witness. There might be some exceptions, but for the most part, every child is an observer of some form of peer abuse. Witnessing bullying without being a participant does not leave a child unscathed. In Chapter Two we highlighted the role of the witness and made recommendations for educators. In this chapter, we want to pinpoint the parent's role.

Encourage your child to take some action to support a target, such as not becoming an audience for a bully or laugh at his/her put-downs. Talk to them about connecting with a positive peer group that won't join forces with a bully for self-protection.

Have a conversation about the difference between tattling and reporting and remind them that reporting is being responsible. Keep communication going and inquire from time to time if they have found a way to reach out to a target who needs support.

Model good witness behavior. Paula Fried, co-author, *Bullies, Targets & Witnesses,* Fried & Fried, described a situation she witnessed when picking up her son from school. She was lined up with all of the other mothers in their vans at curbside when two boys ran out of school, threw their books on the ground and started beating on each other. Paula looked to see if anyone was rushing to their rescue but no such hero appeared. She looked at all of the other mothers who were frozen in their driver's seats and made the decision to intervene.

She strode forcefully to the boys and calmly suggested that they find some other way to settle their dispute. They looked at her quizzically, gathered up their books and left the scene. Paula returned to her car, only to notice that the two boys were now at the street corner, books scattered and exchanging blows. Once again, she walked determinedly to the site of the altercation and tried to reason with the boys about their fighting. Once again, the boys gathered their belongings and this time fled out of sight.

Paula is firmly convinced that her efforts had no effect on "stopping the fight" and that they renewed their punches at some location beyond view. What she did realize was that numerous adults witnessed two boys lashing out at each other but either felt helpless or chose not to intercede. If nothing else, she set an example for responsible witness behavior.

PARENTS AS PARTNERS

If you want to be a solid partner with your school, become the best parent that you can be. In this section, we have gathered helpful research and data for parents who want their children's educational years to be satisfying and successful.

Beginning at birth, take advantage of two extraordinary programs that support new families, if they are available in your community. Parents As Teachers offers its services to any new family and Healthy Families America provides services for parents who need more intense contact. A trained parent educator will work with you during your child's first three years of life. The Parent Educator or Home Visitor serves as a caring coach whose intent is to support you to become the best parent possible.

The American Academy of Pediatrics says children under the age of two shouldn't watch TV at all and that older kids should watch no more than two hours a day. While there is a great deal of conflicting data about media influence, there's little disagreement that violent programs are bad for children, leading to fear and aggressive behavior and that TV in a child's bedroom can lead to sleep disorders.

Be sure to give your children the basic social skills to prepare them for the school socializing experience. By the time children enter kindergarten they should know how to share, how to treat adults with respect, to master basic manners and etiquette, to have a good sense of right and wrong, and how to be kind. Your children will develop and absorb more basic information in the first three to five years of their lives than in any other comparable time period. Before your children ever appear at the school door, your influence on their behavior is firmly imprinted.

Children who feel respected will in turn respect others. The more control they exert over their own actions, the less likely they will need to control others. When you love your children unconditionally and consistently, the sense of security they will receive is priceless.

Teaching children to manage their anger is a critical task of parenting. Families in particular and society in general need to find better ways to deal with anger and rage. Driving habits have cost people their lives and "road rage" has entered our vocabulary. Children need to learn how to express anger appropriately, to calm down when they're ready to explode, and to handle their frustrations and disappointments in healthy ways.

The ability to develop impulse control has surprising power to predict a child's future. "The marshmallow test" consists of challenging a 4 year old to sit at a table with a marshmallow. If the child can wait until an adult comes in the room, s/he will get two marshmallows. If s/he can't wait that long, they just get the one.

An article in the *Boston Globe* by Carey Goldberg, states that the longer the child can hold back, from a minute to 20 minutes, the better the outlook in later life for everything from SAT scores to social skills to academic achievement. Columbia University psychologist, Walter Mischel, has followed his test subjects from preschool in the late 1960s into their 40s now. The ability to delay gratification truly correlates with success in life, according to the research. The fascinating study appeared in the September 2008 edition of *Psychological Science*. There are training techniques that are worth parent curiosity.

Resilience is a topic that has been heavily researched. Emmy E. Werner and Ruth Smith conducted a 30-year study that found identifiable factors that build resilience.

Having an adult mentor is the most significant. Effective reading skills by age 8 was one of the most potent predictors of successful adult adaptation.

Children who were given responsibilities, especially looking out for the welfare of others, fared well. Werner and Smith discovered that social skills advanced popularity, and popular children have more friends, are more confident, cheerful, humorous, and intelligent.

Resilient children know how to find and use information to solve problems. When faced with adversity, they look at many options to deal with their circumstance. Hobbies and interests bring children in contact with more people who can bring comfort and solace in times of stress. Finally, resilient children have hope and plans for the future.

Putting practices in place to help your children develop resiliency will certainly come in handy when bullying situations crop up.

One thing is clear, however you deal with your own emotions when you are distressed, angry, or frustrated will surely be copied by your offspring. As always, being a role model is the most persuasive lecture you will ever give.

Always assume that you are a partner with your children's teachers in their school success. You and the classroom teacher are a double dose of education and protection. No one else will spend more time with your child or understand their triumphs and their quirks. You see your child in the context of your family; the teacher sees your child in the context of a class of 15–30 children, not to mention the years of working with countless other children of the same age. Their observations about your child should be received openly, even when you are learning things unpleasant to hear.

We must acknowledge that there are teachers who are negligent about dealing with bullying situations and even teachers who are bullies themselves. Begin with the teacher, even when unresponsive, and document the failed conversation. Then follow the chain of command.

There is one last stipulation to being a valuable partner with your school. It has to do with the computer. There is universal agreement that children should not have a computer in their bedroom. The extent of tragic electronic bullying has led to unanimous calls for parents to monitor the Internet communication in their home.

Schools are being called upon to deal with the consequences of cyber bullying and cell phone indiscretions that are taking place at home. Parents must step up to the plate and assume supervision for cell phone imprudence and Internet offenses on home computers. Schools can offer educational programs on cyber space bullying and establish and implement consequences for abuses that come to their attention, but parents cannot expect schools to be wholly responsible for the transgressions of their children—any time, anywhere.

As one thoughtful lawyer observed, would we expect the school to be responsible for a fight that occurred between your child and a neighbor in your front yard? At what point can the school be expected to control all damaging behaviors between peers?

PARENTS AS ADVOCATES

Parents can be extremely effective advocates, not only for their own children but for other children as well. You can become involved with your PTA/PTO to make antibullying a year-long priority. You can make the same commitment to your Girl Scout, Boy Scout, Campfire and/or other youth groups. These organizations have access to quality materials, programs, and activities about bullying. Girl Scouts of America has created wonderful resources and sponsored national workshops on bullying prevention. Offer to pay for a qualified speaker to come to your school or weekly meeting or camp. Your support may make the difference in a child's life.

Make your carpool a "no put-down zone." Explain to all of your passengers that there will be no name-calling or rudeness while you are the driver. Share with them how important it is to you that everyone feels physically and emotionally safe when you are their driver.

Make the same rules for sleepovers at your home. No sabotage. One mother learned that her daughter, Trisha, was being invited to a pajama party where some of the girls were going to be subjected to humiliation. The hostess and some of her friends were going to tie their guests' clothing in knots and put their bras in the freezer. Trisha's mom contacted the mother of the hostess and disclosed the plot. The sleepover was cancelled. Initially, Trisha was furious at her mother for interfering. A few of the girls retaliated by shunning Trisha. Ultimately, Trisha realized that she was going to be the brunt of their dirty tricks, one way or the other.

Sports are ripe for bullying. We have been horrified to read about parents who were responsible for the death of an ice-hockey coach or another parent because of their fury about a decision during a game—adult role modeling gone amok.

You will have countless opportunities to discuss the art of winning and losing with your children and to bring reason to bleacher behavior.

One of our favorite stories is the case of a young boy, Ernie, who was uncoordinated and rather nonathletic. Despite his liabilities, he enjoyed playing soccer, and his coach believed that sports were not just about competition. He believed there were skills to be learned—such as teamwork, self-discipline, giving your very best. Every player was given an equal chance to play during the game, regardless of his ability. The parents were thrilled to have a coach with such solid values. That is, everyone but Ernie's Dad, Sonny.

Sonny showed up at every game, that was the good news. The bad news was that whenever Ernie was rotated in and missed a kick, his father stood up in the stands and screamed at him for being "such a slug." "Can't you ever do anything thing right?" "Stop rushing the ball!" Ernie was mortified and the other parents were in agony. They were embarrassed for Ernie and angry at his father but felt helpless to change the situation. They got together and decided not to confront the father, fearing it would make him even more belligerent. Instead, whenever Ernie came on the field, all of the parents cheered him on. They drowned out his father with words of encouragement—"Hang in there, Ernie," "You're doing your best," "Keep trying!" That is parent advocacy at its very best.

Become familiar with your school code of conduct for staff and students. Many schools insist that students and parents read and sign the code of conduct. Your school board should have an antibullying policy and your state should have pertinent legislation. Thirty-eight states have passed antibullying laws and those laws have been rated by an energetic agency, www.bullypolice.com. Check out the legislation that exists or does not exist in your state. If your state is one that does not have antibullying legislation, BullyPoliceUSA would appreciate your involvement to make it happen.

Parent Meeting on Bullying Prevention

Make a special effort to attend any PTA or PTO meetings on the topic of bullying or school safety. Attendance is usually confined to a small group of parents of the targets and the officers of the parent organization. Changing the school culture cannot be borne by those who are in pain alone. One of your children may have a solid social standing but the next one might not. Make a commitment to the ideals of the school community, regardless of the comfort level of your current student.

Offer to be part of a planning committee to capture a wider audience. Recruit a group of fathers to perform a "kindness rap" at the PTA/PTO bullying meeting, with appropriate baseball caps on backwards, et al. Ask the principal to assign the student council to conduct a school survey about bullying issues and give a report of their findings at the meeting. Offer to be part of the hospitality committee who will serve supper or dessert at the event.

Volunteer to assist with recess and/or supervise bus rides on field trips. It will mean a great deal to your sons and daughters and be an enormous boon to the teachers and bus drivers. Be sure to enforce the situational rules.

It is the responsibility of parents to teach manners and etiquette to their children. Basic concepts of respect, courtesy, "please," "may I," "thank you," "pardon me," should be instilled in your children before they ever attend school. A conversation with a teacher who was dealing with an influx of children who had escaped the devastation of Katrina in New Orleans was very informative. She had made an assumption that integrating those students into her classroom was going to be a tremendous chore. To her great surprise, the children always answered her questions with "Yes, ma'am" and "No, ma'am." The gift of politeness enriched all of her students and made learning easier for everyone.

You may not realize that your child is bullying. Listen with an open mind to information that school staff shares with you. Support school polices on antibullying behavior and reinforce those adopted codes of conduct in your own home.

Consider yourself a valuable link in the chain of change agents who believe that change is possible and are passionate about the outcome. Joanne Stern, in her book, *Parenting is a Contact Sport,* gives us wonderful advice—"Build a relationship with your children that's so strong, nothing will sever it. From toddlerhood to teen years and beyond, you can make 'real' contact with your kids, forming an unbreakable bond that makes you the person they want to share with and gives you the opportunity to guide and counsel them in every phase of their lives."

Chapter 12

Resources to Move us into the Future

That's one small step for man; one giant leap for mankind.

—Neil Armstrong

It took thousands of individuals to put a man on the moon, but we did it. It is taking thousands of scientists to find the cure for cancer, diabetes, and many other diseases, but we are doing it. And it will take thousands of professionals and concerned citizens to banish bullying behavior but we can/will do it.

The abundant research literature and anecdotal literature that address the serious societal issue of bullying underscores the need to respond to a call for immediate action. With this book we are trying to heed the call and to help readers do so as well. In this chapter we present additional resources to accomplish the very important task that lies ahead.

VIDEOS AND DVDs

Videos and DVDs are excellent resources for students, teachers, and parents. They can serve as a catalyst for opening the lines of communication between adults and children. School professionals might preview the video they plan to show to their students at a PTA meeting. They could discuss the video with the parents and then give suggestions of how parents might best discuss the video with their children at home.

Early Elementary—Grades K–3

Buddy Learns About Bullying—Marco Products—13 minutes
Presents ways students can avoid being bullied and includes exercises for
    classroom discussion.
Emily Breaks Free—Marsh Media—15 minutes
Presents the issue of bullying from the perspective of a dog.
McGruff's Bully Alert—AIMS Multimedia—15 minutes
Also using a dog, McGruff, students learn how to assert themselves when
    dealing with bullies.
Stop Teasing Me!—Sunburst Media—13 minutes
Three vignettes about bullying portrayed by real students.

Elementary Grades 4–6

Bullies Are A Pain In The Brain—Trevor Romain—25 minute DVD 0212
Could span ages 8–13.
Bullying and How to Handle It: A Video for 3rd & 4th Grades—Hazelden
    Publishing & Educational Services—12 minutes
Students discuss their own bullying experiences and make practical sugges-
    tions on how to deal with bullies.
Push and Shove—Marco Products—25 minutes
A story that explores the feelings of both the bully and the victim.
Broken Toy—National Center for Youth Issues—25 minutes
The story of a 12-year-old boy who is the ongoing target of bullies, who only
    begin to question their behavior when they go too far.

Middle School—Grades 5–9

Peer Pressure—Schlessinger Media—30 minutes
Students discuss the very important topic of peer pressure and present sugges-
    tions as to how best resist negative influences.

High School—Grades 7–12

Bullies & Harassment On Campus—TMW Media Group—21 minutes
Interviews with teenagers on the topic of how they can deal with harassment
    from peers who bully.
Bang, Bang, You're Dead—Paramount Collection—93 minutes
A powerful play within a play about a high school student who is relent-
    lessly tormented by his classmates and becomes involved in a plot to
    seek vengeance. A caring teacher tries to reach out to him and casts him

in a play called "Bang, Bang, You're Dead" about a student who kills his classmates to get revenge.

Let's Get Real—The Respect For All Project—35 minutes

A documentary involving youth who speak up about name-calling and bullying. This film won the Columbine Award for best short documentary.

WEB SITES

We have discussed the global nature of bullying today. These Web sites give you the opportunity to explore bullying around the world as well as in the United States.

www.bullying.co.uk
British Web site for teachers, students, and parents.
www.bullying.org
Canadian Web site for adults on bully prevention and intervention. Also includes stories, drawings, and poems about children's bully experiences.
www.antibullying.net
Located at the University of Edinburgh, Scotland, presents materials for educators, students, and parents about how to deal with bullying.
www.bullyingnoway.com.au
Bullying, No Way! is developed and managed by Australian education authorities for use by Australia's Government, Catholic, and Independent school communities.
www.timesonline.co.uk
Positive parenting guidance to help deal with parenting challenges such as bullying.
www.byparents-forparents.com
Online parenting resources for parents of teens designed to help parents avoid giving their teens mixed messages.

USA Web Sites

www.stopbullyingnow.com.
Take a Stand, Lend a Hand, Stop Bullying Now! offers an amazing array of resources in every conceivable form of communication. Sponsored by the Health Resources and Services Administration, a Division of the Department of Health and Human Services, this campaign made its debut in 2004. It is continually updated to provide significant information about

bullying to students, parents, and youth serving organizations. Student input has always been an important element and ensures its relevance. Materials are also available in Spanish.

CHILDREN'S LITERATURE

Children's Literature is an integral part of the curriculum in virtually all schools. It is an excellent source and vehicle for teaching and discussing the many aspects of bullying we have covered in this book. Following are several school activities using children's literature that are very successful and some books for recommended reading.

Teacher Reading Aloud

Strange as it may seem, children of all ages enjoy listening to their teachers read chapter books aloud. Many teachers read chapter books after lunch as a transition to the afternoon classes. Teachers often select books to elicit discussion on topics of interest and concern such as bullying. Book suggestions include early childhood books as well as chapter books.

Grades preschool–1

Agassi, M. Hands Are Not for Hitting. Minneapolis: Free Spirit, 2000.
Estes, E. The Hundred Dresses. Hong Kong: Voyager Book, 1944, 1972.
Thomas, P., Harker, L. Stop Picking On Me: A First Look at Bullying. Hauppauge, NY: Barron's Educational Series, 2000.

Grades 2–5

Otoshi, K. One. California: K O Kids Books, 2008.
Pike, K., Mumper, J., Fiske, A. Teaching Kids to Care and Cooperate. New York: Scholastic, 2000.
O'Neill, A. The Recess Queen. New York: Scholastic, 2002

Grades 5–12

Miller, D. Time to Tell'Em Off! A Pocket Guide to Overcoming Peer Ridicule. Merrifield, VA: Deanna Miller, 2000.

Fiction

Berenstein, S., Berenstein, J. The Berenstein Bears and Too Much Teasing. New York: Random House, 1995.

Carlson, N. Loudmouth George and the Sixth-Grade Bully. Minneapolis: Carolrhoda Books, 2003.

Junior Great Books Discussion

Many teachers and some parent volunteers are certified to lead Junior Great Books discussions. Most of the books on our recommended reading list would be very effective for Junior Great Books discussions. This format promotes active participation by all students and forces them to really probe a topic such as bullying.

The following classics follow in the Junior Great Books tradition:

Polacco, P. Thank you, Mr. Falker. New York: Philomel Books, 1998.
Shange, N. Whitewash. New York: Walker and Company, 1997.
White, E.B. Charlotte's Web. New York: Harper Collins, 1974.

Book Reviews/Reports

Each student in the class would choose a book from this list to read and then give an oral report. The students are challenged to present their report with the goal of convincing their classmates to also read their book. The student who convinces the most classmates to read his/her book receives a prize. Students enjoy the competition and can be very creative in their presentations. These book reports are an effective springboard for meaningful bully discussions.

Appropriate Reading Levels

In many classes students are on different reading levels. Our recommended reading list includes books at various levels. Teachers should guide their students to read books at their appropriate level, the independent level if no reading instruction will take place and the instructional level if there will be teacher reading instruction during the course of the student's reading of the book.

Grades K–4

Johnston, M. Dealing with Bullying. Center City, MN: Hazelden, 1998.
Brown, M. T. Arthur's April Fool. Boston: Little, Brown, 1985.
Powell, J. Talking About Bullying. Chicago: Raintree, 1999.

Grades 2–8

Kaufman, G., Esplande, P., Raphael, L. Stick Up for Yourself. Minneapolis, MN: Free Spirit Publishing, Inc., 1999.

Romain, T. Bullies Are a Pain in the Brain. Minneapolis, MN: Free Spirit Publishing, Inc., 1995.

Cohen-Posey, K. How to Handle Bullies, Teasers, and Other Meanies: A Book that Takes the Nuisance Out of Name Calling and Other Nonsense. Lake Zurich, IL: Rainbow Books, 1995.

Eberly, S. 365 Manners Kids Should Know: Games, Activities, and Other Fun Ways to Help Children Learn Etiquette. New York: Three Rivers Press, 2001.

Fried, S., Lang, L. 30 Activities for Getting Better at Getting Along, www.bullysafe.usa.com 2005.

Sacher, L. There's a Boy in the Girl's Bathroom. New York: Random House, 1987.

Romain, T. Cliques, Phonies & Other Baloney. Minneapolis: MN. Free Spirit Publishing, 1998.

Grades 7–12

Appleman, D. Always Use Protection: A Teen's Guide to Safe Computing. Berkeley: Apress, 2004.

Blanco, Jodee. Please Stop Laughing at Me . . . One Woman's Inspirational Story. Avon, MA: Adams Media Corporation, 2003.

Books for Teen Girls

Mosatche, H., Lawner, E.K. Ask Dr. M and Liz about friends, family, guys and more ... New York: Girl Scouts of the United States of America, 2005.

Mosatche, H.S., Lawner, E.K. Getting to Know the Real You 50—Fun Quizzes Just for Girls. New York: Three Rivers Press, 2002.

Mosatche, H.S. Girls: What's so Bad About Being Good? How to Have Fun, Survive the Preteen Years, And Remain True to Yourself. New York: Three Rivers Press, 2001.

Books for Adults

Berkley, B., Economy, P. Giving Back. New Jersey: John Wiley & Sons, 2008.

Cornelius, H., Faire, S., with Cornelius, S. Everyone Can Win—Responding to Conflict Constructively. Second Edition. Australia: Simond & Schuster, 2006.

Cullen, D. Columbine. New York: Hachette Book Group, 2009.

Elman, N., Kennedy-Moore, E. The Unwritten Rules of Friendship. Eugene, Org.: Harvest House Publishers, 2003.

Fried, S., Fried, P. Bullies & Victims—Helping Your Child Through the Schoolyard Battlefield. New York: M. Evans and Company, 1996.

Fried, S., Fried, P. Bullies, Targets & Witnesses—Helping Children Break the Pain Chain. New York: M. Evans and Company, 2003.

Garbarino, J., deLara, E. And Words Can Hurt Forever—How to Protect Adolescents from Bullying, Harassment, and Emotional Violence. New York: Free Press, 2001.

Garbarino, J. See Jane Hit—Why Girls Are Growing More Violent and What We Can Do About It. New York: Penguin Books, 2007.

Gladwell, M. The Tipping Point, How Little Things Can Make A Big Difference. Boston: Little Brown and Company, 2000.

Gossen, D. It's all about WE—Rethinking Discipline Using Restitution. Saskatoon: Chelsom Consultants Limited, 2004.

Phillips, R., Linney, J., Pack, C. Safe School Ambassadors: Harnessing Student Power to Stop Bullying and Violence. Champaign: Research Press, 2008.

Stern, J. Parenting is a Contact Sport. Austin: Greenleaf Book Group, 2009.

Underwood, J. Today I Made a Difference. Avon, MA: Adams Media Corp., 2009.

ORGANIZATIONS AND AGENCIES

There are outstanding organizations from coast to coast and worldwide producing research, model programs, training materials, curricula, information on prevention and intervention of bullying, and help for parents, educators, school counselors and psychologists, as well as school administrators. Some produce videos and all have Web sites.

Anti-Bullying Centre at Trinity College in Dublin, Ireland
Dr. Mona O'Moore, Director
Tel: (01)876-2573/876-3488
E-mail: lmcquire@tcd.ie
Web site: www.abc.tcd.ie/school.htm

The Centre offers a resource reference library, advice, and guidance by phone or in person for researchers, parents, teachers, schools, and organizations; research advice and survey assistance for individuals, schools, and organizations; counseling services, in-service, and staff development for schools and organizations; and conferences and workshops for pupils, parents, and teachers.

BullySafeUSA
4003 Homestead Drive
Shawnee Mission, Kansas 66208
Tel: (913)362-2226 FAX: (913)362-5540
E-mail: suellenfried@hotmail.com
Web site: www.bullysafeusa.com

BullySafeUSA, a research-based bullying prevention program, founded by
SuEllen Fried, offers a range of services, including student empowerment
sessions with students grades K–12, in-service staff training, conference
keynote speeches and workshops, parent seminars, and a three-day Training
the Trainer Institute. The vision of the organization is to change the school
culture to become a caring, compassionate, and kind environment.

Character Education Partnership
1025 Connecticut Avenue, Suite 1011
Washington, D.C. 20036
Tel: (800)988-8081
www.character.org

Provides information and resources on character education. Web site has links
to research reports, curricula, and their "Character Education Newsletter."

Character Plus
A Division of Cooperating School Districts
1460 Craig Road
St. Louis, MO 63146
KrusorDavis@earthlink.net
Tel: (417)334-1188

Character Plus works with schools districts in Missouri to develop a comprehensive program for students, parents, and the community on character traits.
The Show-Me initiative will give guidance to schools who want to emphasize
character development.

Girl Scouts USA
420 Fifth Ave., 9th Floor
New York, NY 10018
Tel: (800)478-7248
(212)852-8000
www.girlscouts.org.

Girl Scouts of the USA is the world's most preeminent organization dedicated solely to girls. They offer a wealth of materials, books, and videos to help girls build character and skills for success in the real world. They focus on developing leadership skills, strong values, and a social conscience.

Healthy Families America
A Division of Prevent Child Abuse America
500 S. Michigan Ave. Suite 200
Chicago, IL 60611
Tel: (312)663-2250
www.preventchildabuse.org

Healthy Families America is a national program model designed to help expectant and new parents get their children off to a healthy start. Families participate voluntarily in the program and receive home visiting services from trained staff for children from birth to three years of age.

I-SAFE America
5963 La Place Court, Suite 309
Carlsbad, CA 92008
Tel: (760)603-7911
www.isafe.org

A not-for-profit Internet foundation that focuses on computer safety information and awareness for students K–12. Provides curriculum for schools, free of charge, in all 50 states.

National Conference for Community and Justice of Metropolitan St. Louis
Anytown Youth Leadership Institute
4609 Shaw Blvd. Suite 142
St. Louis, Mo 63110
Tel: (314)865-3042
nccjstl@sbcglobal.net
www.nccjst.org

The Anytown Youth Leadership Institute is designed to expose young people of all races, religions, and cultures to multicultural issues and topics and facilitate purposeful intergroup dialogue on addressing systemic oppression and privilege. The Retreat format engages high school students in a process to change attitudes and to gain insights regarding prejudice, bias, and stereotypes.

National School Safety Center
141 Duesenberg Drive, Suite 11
Westlake Village, CA 91362
Tel: (805)373-9977 Fax: (805)373-9277
www.schoolsafety.us

The NSSC serves as an advocate for safe, secure, and peaceful schools world-wide and as a catalyst for the prevention of school crime and violence.

National Social Norms Institute (NSNI)
University of Virginia
943 Second Street, S.E.
Charlottesville, VA 22902
Tel: (434)982-6688
smc2j@virginia.edu
www.socialnorms.org

The social norms approach in the field of health promotions uses a variety of methods to correct negative misperceptions (usually overestimations) and to identify, model, and promote the healthy, protective behaviors that are the actual norm in a given population.

Olweus Bullying Prevention Program
Institute on Family and Neighborhood Life
Clemson University
Clemson, South Carolina 29631
Tel: (864)710-4562
Fax: (406)862-8971
nobullly@clemson.edu
www.olweus.org.

The Olweus bullying prevention program is an evidence-based, comprehensive, school-wide program designed for use in elementary, middle, or junior high schools. The goals are to reduce and prevent bullying problems and to improve peer relations at school.

Ophelia Project
718 Nevada Drive
Erie, PA 16505
Tel: (814)456-5437
Ophelia@opheliaproject.org.
www.opheliaproject.org.

The Ophelia Project serves youth and adults who are affected by relational aggression by providing them with a unique combination of tools, strategies, and solutions. The goal is to achieve long-term systemic change.

Parents as Teachers National Center, Inc.
2228 Ball Drive
St. Louis, Mo. 63146
Tel: (866)728-4968 toll free
(314)432-4330
Fax: (314)432-8963
info@parentsasteachers.org.
www.parentsasteachers.org

Parents as Teachers provides parent educators for families with newborns who request the service. The program continues for the first three years of life in partnership with local school districts. The vision is to support parents to become the very best first teachers for their children and prepare them for a successful learning experience in school.

Reaching Out From Within
P.O. Box 8527
Prairie Village, KS 66208
Tel: (913)681-2605
reachinmatesks@aol.com
www.reachinmatesks.com
www.reachinmatesks.org.

Reaching Out From Within is a self-help program for inmates in seven Kansas Correctional Facilities. This transformational self-help program for male and female inmates was founded in 1982. Members of the program meet weekly to learn alternative ways to deal with violence and stress in order to become productive family members and citizens when they are released. The recidivism rate is 8.9 percent as compared to a national recidivism rate of 50 percent.

Steps to Respect
Committee for Children
568 First Avenue South Suite 600
Seattle, WA 98104
Tel: (800)634-4449
www.cfchildren.org

Steps to Respect, along with Second Step, is a research-based social and emotional learning program that promotes school success and teaches critical skills in bullying prevention, empathy and communication, and emotional management. The program offers easy-to-use tools, lesson plans, and a school wide implementation support kit.

Strong American Schools
1150 17th Street, NW 8th Floor
Washington, D.C., 20036
Tel: (202)552-4560
www.strongamericanschools.org

Strong American Schools has produced a policy toolkit to bring about much needed change in our public schools. The three areas covered in the toolkit are American Education Standards, Effective Teachers in Every Classroom, and Expanded Time and Support for Learning.

Teaching Tolerance Educational Program
A Division of the Southern Poverty Law Center
400 Washington Ave.
Montgomery, AL 36104
Tel: (334)956-8200 Fax: (334)956-8488
Web site: www.Tolerance.org

Classroom resources include a magazine, curriculum kits, films, and books. Many of the materials are free, and there are discounts for bulk orders. The magazine *Teaching Tolerance* is published twice a year. It profiles K–12 educators, schools, and programs that are promoting diversity and equity in inspirational and replicable ways.

Teach for America
West 36th Street
7th Floor
New York, NY 10018
Tel: (800)832-1230
(212)279-2080
Fax: (212)279-2081
www.teachforamerica.org

Teach for America is the national corps of outstanding recent college graduates and professionals of all academic majors and career interests who commit two years to teach in urban and rural public schools and become leaders in the effort to expand educational opportunity.

Appendix A

Discussion Questions for Book Groups and PTA Discussion Groups and/or Meetings

Discuss the authors' definition of bullying and bullying behavior and relate it to your own experiences with and/or concept of bullying.

Do you share the authors' observation that "bullying is a learned behavior, acquired primarily from family members and/or friends"? If so, how can this cycle be broken?

How can the media influence on violence be stopped? Should concerned citizens take an active role in this, and if so where to start?

Discuss your experience with the cycle of pain, rage, and revenge and relate it to the authors' presentation of this cycle.

Discuss the authors' recommendations for changing the culture. Which of these recommendations do you think would be most effective in your school/ community? How do you think they can best be implemented?

How well are the schools in your community monitoring physical, verbal, emotional, sexual, and cyber bullying? Are parents, school personnel, and law enforcement in your community adequately alert to the dangers of cyber bullying?

How are they addressing this serious social issue?

How well does your school/community address the needs of special needs students? What recommendations in this book did you find the most helpful? Discuss additional suggestions you might have.

How can you as individuals and as a group be effective change agents?

Which of the Ten Burning Questions are your most burning questions? Why?

How do you relate to the role of parents as discussed in the book? Do you see any additional roles parents might have in banishing bully behavior?

What has been your experience with the various developmental stages of bullying behavior? Do you agree with the authors about the importance of teaching and modeling social skills in order to create a positive environment at school and at home?

Appendix B

Introduction

This section is designed to serve as a guide for Educators and College/University Students but it can be helpful to the lay reader as well. It can also be used for In-service training sessions and professional development. The Anticipatory Set should help every reader, professional and lay, focus on the material covered in each chapter. The Beyond the Text gives the reader the opportunity for hands on experiences and to go beyond the text to the real world.

CHAPTER ONE—THE DYNAMICS OF PAIN, RAGE & REVENGE

Anticipatory Set

1. Have you experienced the cycle of pain, rage and revenge? If so, how did you handle it?
2. How would you break the cycle of pain, rage and revenge?
3. Can you give an example from your own experience when "belief trumped reason"?

Beyond the Text

1. Share an article from the Internet that gives you additional insight into the cycle of pain, rage and revenge.
2. Discuss the cycle of pain, rage and revenge with a health care professional.
3. Prepare a lesson plan to help your students understand pain, rage and revenge and the importance of breaking the cycle.

CHAPTER TWO—DIMENSIONS AND OVERVIEW OF BULLYING

Anticipatory Set

1. Are there some valuable life lessons that children can learn from bullying experiences or is bullying always negative?
2. Is bullying more severe today than it was fifty years ago?
3. What is the correlation between bullying and other serious social problems?
4. According to the authors is bullying a childhood rite of passage or is it a form of child abuse?

Beyond the Text

1. Explore the Internet and find a site that is an indication of the global nature of bullying in the 21st century.
2. Relate the information in this chapter to your own knowledge and experience as a student and as a pre-service teacher.
3. Journal your reactions to this chapter.

CHAPTER THREE—BACK TO BULLYING BASICS

Anticipatory Set

1. How does the text definition of bullying and bullying behavior concur with your own experience with and/or concept of bullying?
2. Consider what information in this chapter you find to be most informative, most surprising, most relevant and most useful.
3. Why is the term target considered more appropriate than the term victim in relation to the bully?

Beyond the Text

1. Find an Internet site posted after the publication of this text that brings new and/or additional information to what you learned in Chapter 3. Share this with your class/colleagues.
2. Prepare a lesson plan that is age/grade appropriate to teach the information in this chapter which students must know to stop bullying behavior.

3. Interview a classroom teacher to learn his/her experience with the information in this chapter. Have your questions prepared before you go to the interview.

CHAPTER FOUR—HOW CAN I HURT THEE? LET ME COUNT THE WAYS

Anticipatory Set

1. What new information about the five types of bullying have you learned from this chapter that will be important for you to know as a classroom teacher/parent?
2. As a pre-service teacher (or a graduate student in education) have you observed any of these types of bullying during your field experiences?
3. Does this chapter give you any ideas of how you might prevent bullying in your classroom?

Beyond the Text

1. Select a current article from the Internet that will expand your knowledge about cyber bullying.
2. Talk with someone in law-enforcement about cyber bullying. How well are they working with the schools to keep students safe from cyber bullies?
3. How well prepared do you feel as a teacher to see that your students can thrive in a bully free classroom? What additional support might you need?

CHAPTER FIVE—PERSPECTIVES ON THE BULLYING CONTINUUM

Anticipatory Set

1. Why is early intervention so important during early childhood education to prevent bullying behavior to continue?
2. Discuss the predictive nature of middle childhood with your colleagues.
3. Read to learn more about the serious lifelong consequences of bullying behavior.

Beyond the Text

1. Explore a web site concerning the developmental stage in which you plan to teach.

2. Visit a classroom at the developmental stage level of your choice and observe the students' behavior. Does the behavior match what you would expect after having read this chapter?
3. Using some of the resources presented in Chapter 12 learn more about the developmental stage of your choice.

CHAPTER SIX—HELPING STUDENTS WITH SPECIAL NEEDS ACHIEVE SUCCESS

Anticipatory Set

1. Read to learn more about the medication debate.
2. According to the authors, why is it more important to show special needs students that they can be successful than to tell them that you know that they can be successful?
3. Why are "twice exceptional students" considered to be "at risk"?

Beyond the Text

1. Find a current article on the Internet about the medication debate that gives you new information since the publication of this book.
2. Learn to use some of the instruments for student evaluation discussed in this chapter.
3. Start to collect materials that will help you work with special needs students.

CHAPTER SEVEN—THE CHALLENGE OF CHANGING THE CULTURE

Anticipatory Set

1. What information in this chapter do you think you can use to change the culture in which you are or will be working?
2. Read to learn about the grass roots movement among prevention educators called "social norming."
3. Why do you think the Kindness programs are so effective?

Beyond the Text

1. Select a web site to learn more about changing the culture.

2. Observe a Kindness program and evaluate its effectiveness.
3. Journal your reactions to the recommendations for changing the culture discussed in this chapter.
4. Outline your ideas for changing the culture in your school.

CHAPTER EIGHT—CHANGE AGENTS

Anticipatory Set

1. In the school(s) you are familiar with how many of the Change Agents follow the recommendations discussed in this chapter?
2. How would you prioritize the recommendations made in this chapter?
3. Which Change Agent in the community at large do you think can be the most helpful and effective in bringing about meaningful change in the culture with respect to bullying behavior?

Beyond the Text

1. Find a web site that gives you additional information about Change Agents.
2. Interview one of the Change Agents in the school community and share what you learn with your classmates/colleagues. Prepare your list of questions in writing based on what you learned in this chapter before the interview.
3. Meet with one of the Change Agents in the community at large to discuss what you learned in this chapter and ask for some feedback from his/her perspective. Share what you learn with your classmates/colleagues.

CHAPTER NINE—ENGAGING THE STUDENTS IN THE SOLUTION

Anticipatory Set

1. Read to learn about the key components of the Student Empowerment Session (SES) that make it so effective.
2. Which of the research studies did you find the most informative?
3. What did you find the most enlightening about the Student Empowerment Session?

Beyond the Text

1. Explore the BullySafeUSA web site.

2. Observe a Student Empowerment Session.
3. Take the SES training.

CHAPTER TEN—TEN BURNING QUESTIONS POSED BY EDUCATORS

Anticipatory Set

1. Which of these ten burning questions are burning questions for you?
2. What has made them burning questions for you?
3. If some are not burning questions for you, how have you resolved them?
4. Do you have any additional burning questions? If so – what are they?

Beyond the Text

1. Choose your most burning question and find a satisfactory answer on the Internet.
2. How would you respond to each of these ten most burning questions?
3. Discuss these ten most burning questions with your classmates/colleagues. Journal answers that you might find helpful at a later date.
4. Choose one of these most burning questions and pose it to an educator whose professionalism you respect and value.

CHAPTER ELEVEN—PARENTS AS PROTECTORS, PARTNERS AND ADVOCATES

Anticipatory Set

1. Read to learn how to empower your child/student to manage his/her own bullying problem.
2. Why is it important for your child to know that you are willing to go up the chain of command on his/her behalf?
3. What enables parents to be protectors, partners and advocates?
4. What makes these parent roles so vital for the welfare of the child, the school and the community in order to banish bullying behavior?

Beyond the Text

1. There are many informative web sites to help parents deal with bullying. Select one and share it with your classmates/colleagues.

2. Prepare a Parent Newsletter that you might use for the parents of your students.
3. Discuss how you might use email to communicate with the parents of your students.

CHAPTER TWELVE—RESOURCES TO MOVE US INTO THE FUTURE

Anticipatory Set

1. Which of these resources do you find most helpful? Why?
2. Which of these resources are available to you?
3. What types of substitutes might you make for some of the resources that are not available to you?

Beyond the Text

1. Use the Internet to find additional resources in an area of special interest to you. Share this information with your classmates/colleagues.
2. Make a file with easy access of the resources you plan to use.
3. Meet with a director of media instruction to find additional resources in an area of special interest to you.

Appendix C

Suggested Format for Class Parents Meeting

As an "icebreaker" to open the meeting you might invite each parent to turn to the parent sitting next to him or her and "interview" him or her for a few minutes and then reverse roles. Rather than going around the room and having each person introduce him or her self everyone introduces the person they interviewed. We also recommend that seating be set up in a circle rather than theater style,

The agenda for the meeting should include

- Explanation of the concept of a community of learners. This should set a nonthreatening tone for the meeting. Discuss the learning environment you are trying to establish for their children.
- Discuss the importance of having a bully free classroom. Give the parents some background on the concept of peer abuse, characteristics of bullies and ask the parents to be honest with themselves as to whether they see any of these characteristics in their own child.
- Discuss the importance of working in cooperation with the home and your commitment to do so. In order for this to work stress to the parents that you need their help. Point out that the research shows the more cooperation between the home and school the more successful the student and that you know that the parents want to help their children achieve success.
- Also discuss the fact that many parents don't realize that their child is either a bully or being bullied and therefore it is important for them to know what to look for and how to help their child overcome being a bully or bullied.

The following questions might be presented in the form of a checklist for the parents to ask themselves:

Does your child:

- Enjoy spreading rumors
- Get pleasure from taunting others
- Seek power over others
- Act out anger in physical ways (hitting, kicking, damaging property)
- Use words to hurt or humiliate others
- Try to isolate his/her target
- Play on other's insecurity
- Is your to recognize the rights of others
- Fail Lack empathy
- Fail to admit mistakes and correct them
- Lack a sense of humor
- Need to be controlling
- Become hot tempered
- Have family problems and issues
- Witness abusive behavior

As part of the discussion you might ask parents to add to the list. Then the discussion should turn to constructive suggestions for addressing these characteristics. Have a list of tools parents can use and explain how you address these issues. Again, asking for parental support and indicating your support for parental actions is very important.

If the class meeting or the meeting with a member of the administrative staff is not an option for you then the only choice you have is a one-on-one meeting with the parents. It might be helpful for you to speak with your student to ascertain his/her parents' interests such as sports, hunting, fishing, music to try to find an area of mutual interest to talk about before you start your discussion on the topic of bullying.

Appendix D

Assessment of Letter Name Knowledge

This is an example of a very simple instrument that can be administered by parents or teachers to assess whether the student can recognize all the letters of the alphabet. You can duplicate this set of letters or make up one of your own. The key is not to have the letters in alphabetical order and to include all 26 letters, upper case and lower case. We also suggest that you not put the lower case b and d next to each other nor the p and q.

Have two copies of the letters, one for the student to read from and one for you to mark any errors by putting a "x" through the letter and writing the letter name the student said instead next to it.

Ask the student to please read the letters to you. If the student should ask you whether s/he should read across or down respond "Any way you want." Then put an arrow in the direction that the student read, across or down. If the student reads down it may indicate that directionality (automatically reading across) has not been firmly established and is another subskill of reading that needs practice.

Any letters that are missed must be retaught, one at a time. The most common problems are confusion of b and d and p and q. Each letter should be retaught until mastered and then the next letter retaught.

ASSESSMENT OF LETTER NAME KNOWLEDGE

O H D U F E

A G S T W Z

X L R I N B

C Y P J V Q M K

m h g k w j

q v y a z u

b l c e n s

o d x f i t r p

References

American Medical Association (2008). "Violence in the media." *National Advisory Council on Violence and Abuse*

Bale, J., (2004). "Parents of bullies are desperate for help." Retrieved 10/26/08 from http://www.timesonline.co.uk/tol/news/uk/article39389 2.ece

Bagley, C., and Tremblay, P. (1997). "Suicidal behavior in homosexual and bisexual males." *American Journal of Public Health.*

Barros, R.M., Silver, E.J., Stein, E.K. (2009). "School recess and group classroom behavior." *Pediatrics* 2/1/09

Bonanno, G.A. (2004). "Loss, trauma, and human resilience – have we underestimated the human capacity to thrive after extremely aversive events?" *American Psychologist* 59 (1) (p. 20–28).

Boulden, W.T. (2006) "Youth leadership, racism, and intergroup dialogue." *Journal of Ethnic & Cultural Diversity in Social Work* 15 (1/2)

Carter, S. (1998). *Civility: manners, morals and the etiquette of democracy.* New York: Harper Collins.

Centers for Disease Control and Prevention. (2007). *Morbidity & Mortality Report.*

Craig, W., and Pepler, D. (1997). "Observations of bullying and victimization in the school yard." *Canadian Journal of School Psychology,* 13 (2) 41–59.

Crary, D. (2009). "Report: Most states lag with dating-violence laws." Retrieved 3/24/09 from http://news.yahoo.com/s/ap/20090324/ap_on_us/

Cortina, L., Magley, V., William, J., and Langhout, R. (2001) "Incivility in the workplace: Incidence and impact." *Journal of Occupational Health Psychology.*

Costello, J. (2004). "Sibling bullying." *Journal of Child Psychology and Psychiatry.*

Cullen, D. (2009). *Columbine.* New York: Hachette Book Group.

Dodge, K., and Coie, J. (1987) "Social information processing factors in reactive and proactive aggression in children's peer groups." *Journal of Personality and Social Psychology.*

Dubow, F. (2009) toledoblade.com. Retrieved 1/29/09 from http://wwwtoledoblade .com/apps/pbcs.dll/article?AID=/20061113/.

Duncan, R.D. (1999). "Peer and sibling aggression: An investigation of intra- and extra-familial bullying. *Journal of Interpersonal Violence* 14 (8).

Education Week, (2008). "Diplomas Count 2008: School to College, Can StateP-16 Councils Ease the Transition?" Bethesda, MD. *Editorial Projects in Education Research Center.*

Elias, M. (2002). "Kids' meanness might mean health risks when they grow up." *USA TODAY,* 9/26.

Espelage, D., and Swearer, S.M. (2004). *Bullying in American schools—a social-ecological perspective on prevention and intervention.* New Jersey: Lawrence Erlbaum Associates, Inc.

Espelage, D.L.(2007) *Bullying in Early Childhood.* Retrieved 11/18/08 from http:// illinoisearlylearning.org/askanexpert/eespelage/trans.htm.

Finkelhor, D., Turner, H., Ormrod, R. (2006). "Kid's stuff: the nature and impact of peer and sibling violence on younger and older children." *Child Abuse & Neglect* 30 (12).

Fried, S. and Fried, P. (1996). *Bullies & victims-helping your child through the schoolyard battlefield.* New York: M. Evans and Company.

Fried, S., and Fried, P. (2003). *Bullies, targets & witnesses—helping children break the pain chain.* New York: M. Evans and Co.

Galinsky, E., and Salmond, K. (2002). "Youth and violence: Students speak out for a more civil society." *Families and Work Institute.*

Garbarino, J., and deLara, E. (2002) *And words can hurt forever.* New York: Free Press.

Garbarino, J. (2006). *See Jane hit—why girls are growing more violent and what we can do about it.* Penguin Press.

Gilligan, C., (1982*). In a different voice.* Harvard University Press.

Gossen, D. (2004) *It's all about WE—rethinking discipline using restitution.* Canada Chelsom Consultants Limited.

Hammond-Darling, L. (2008). 'How they do it abroad." *Time magazine,* 2/25/08, pg. 34.

Harris, J.R. (1999) *The Nurture Assumption.* Florida: Touchstone Books.

High, B., Ed. (2007). "Bullycide in America, moms speak out about the bullying suicide. *JBS Publishing, Inc.*

Hillman, C.B. (1995). *Before the school bell rings.* Portsmouth: Heinemann Publishers.

Horne, R.H., and Sugai, G. (2005). "School-wide positive behavior support: An alternative approach to discipline in schools." *Positive Behavior Support.* New York: Guilford Press

Huebner, A. (2002). "Adolescent Bullying. Virginia Cooperative Extension." Publication Number 350852, Retrieved 2/7/09 from http://www.ext.vt.edu/pubs/ family/350-852/350-852.html.

Husemann, L. R., Eron, L., Lefkowitz, M.M., Walder, L.O. (1984). "Stability of aggression over time and generations." *Developmental Psychology.* 20 (6).

Huston, A., and Ripke, M. Eds. (2006). *Development contexts of middle childhood.* Cambridge: Cambridge University Press.

KIPP. (2009). "What is a KIPP School?" Retrieved 2/7/09 from http://kipp.org/01/whatisakippschool.cfm.

Ingersoll, R.M. (2002). "High turnover plagues schools." *USA TODAY,* 8/15/02.

Johnson, J., Cohen, P., Smailes, F., Kasen, S., and Brook, J. (2002). "Television viewing and aggressive behavior during adolescence and adulthood." *Science* 295 (5564).

Jordan, W.J., Lara, J., McPartland, J.M. (1996). "Exploring the causes of early dropout among race, ethnic and gender groups." *Youth and Society.*

Kowalski, R.M., Limber, S.P., Agatson, P.W. (2007). *Cyber bullying: bullying in the digital age.* Blackwell Publishing.

Laidman, J. (2006). "Is age 8 too late? Kids who don't play well with others may not be successful adults." toledoblade.com. Retrieved 1/29/09 from http://toledoblade.com/apps/pbcs/dll/article?AID=/20061113/.

Landry, D. (2008). "The utilization of creative expression as a means for bullying prevention while creating a respectful environment." Paper delivered at 5th Annual Conference of the International Bullying Prevention Association, Indianapolis, IN. November 6, 7, 2008.

McCaffety, E. (2006). "Bullies online and in chat rooms." National Teen Dating Abuse Helpline. Retrieved 11/18/08 from loveisrespect.org.

Mysilk, L. (2008). "Connect With Kids: Weekly News Stories: Grade School Bullying." Retrieved 11/13/08 from http://www.connectwithkids.com/tipsheet/2008/394_jul 16/thisweek.

NEA Health Information Network. (2005). Statistics: "Gun Violence in Our Communities." 7/14/08 from http://www.neahin.org/programs/schoolsafety/gunsafety/statistics.htm.

Menninger, K. A. (1971). *The Human Mind* (3rd edition). New York: Alfred A. Knopf Nansel, T.R., Overpeck, M., Pilla, R., Ruan, W.J., Simons-Morton, B., Scheidt, P. (2001).

"Bullying behaviors among U.S. youth: Prevalence and association with psychosocial adjustment." *Journal of the American Medical Association,* 285 (16).

Nickelodeon and the Kaiser Family Fund. (2000-01). "Talking with kids." National Survey of Parents and Kids, survey conducted between 12/9/2000 and 1/18/01.

Olweus, D., (1993) *Bullying at school, what we know and what we can do.* Oxford, England: Blackwell Publishers.

Organization for Economic Cooperation and Development. (2008). "Education at a Glance 2008." OECD Indicators. Indicator A1 and A2. Paris, France: OECD Publications. Retrieved from http://www.oecd.org/document/9/0,3343,en 2649 39263238 412667611 1 1 1,00.html.

Parker-Pope, T. (2009) "What are friends for, a longer life." New York Times, 4/2/09.

Peterson, J., and Ray, K.E. (2006). "Bullying among the gifted: The subjective experience." *Gifted Child Quarterly.*

Posey-Cohen, A. (1995). *How to handle bullies, teasers & other meanies.* Florida: Rainbow Books.

Public Agenda. (1999) "Kids these days '99: What Americans really think about the next generation." *Public Agenda.*

Riley, P. (2004). "Five years after Columbine: Students take the lead to stop school violence." *National S.A.V.E.*

Roche, T. (2001). "Voices from the cell" *Time magazine,* 157, (21) 5/28/01.

Sager, N.W., and Garrity, C. (2008). "Bully prevention in early childhood education: Collaboration between teachers and families." article_print http://www.earlychildhoodnews./earlychildhood/article_print.aspx?ArticleID=736 Retrieved 10/16/2008Sager, N.W.

Selman, R., and Demorest, A. (1984). "Observing troubled children's interpersonal negotiation strategies: implications of and for a developmental model." *Child Development,* 55 (1).

Shore, K., (2005). *The ABC's of Bullying Prevention.* New York: Dude Publishing.

Shriver, T., and Weissberg, R.P. (2005). "No emotion left behind." *New York Times,* 8/16/05.

Strong American Schools. (2006). Retrieved January 21, 2009 from www.strong-americanscools.org.

The American Academy of Child & Adolescent Psychiatry. (2008). *Bullying* (No. 80). Retrieved 2/7/09 from http://www.aacap.org/page.ww?name=Bullying&section=Facts.

The Montessori School of Tokyo. (2009). "Sunshine: Goals." Retrieved 1/26/09 from http://montessorijapan.com/Index,php/sp-goals.

Toppo, G. (2009). "Profound shift in home schooling." *USA TODAY,* 5/29-31/09.

Turgade, M., and Fredrickson, B.L. (2004) "Resilient individuals use positive emotions to bounce back from negative emotional experiences." *Journal of Personality and Social Psychology.* 86 (2) p. 320–333.

U.S. Department of Education (2005-06) Common core of data.

Vossekuil, B., Fein, R., Reddy, M., Borum, R., Modzeleski, W. (2004). *The final report of the safe school initiative.* U.S. Department of Education/U.S. Secret Service.

Wepman, J.M., Reynolds, W.M. (1987). *Wepman's Auditory Discrimination Test (ADT).* (2nd Ed.) Los Angeles: Western Psychological Services.

Wheelock, W., and Silvaroli, N., Campbell, C. (2008). *The classroom reading inventory.* (11th Ed.) New York: McGraw Hill.

Wiehe, V.R., (1997) *Sibling abuse, what parents need to know about.* Utah: Bonneville Books.

Wilborn, D. (2008) "Adolescent bullying." Retrieved 1/30/09 from http:www.accessnorthga.com/detail.php?n=209766.

Wilson, J. (1995). *The moral sense.* New York: Free Press, Division of Simon & Schuster.

World Health Organization (1989). *World health statistics.*

Index